DIVINE FIRE

The Book of the Future:
Past & Future Lives, Changing Our Time
Line

Continuing the journey of a soul ...

by
Paulinne Delcour-Min

For permission, serialization, condensation, adaptions, or for our catalog of other publications, write to Ozark Mountain Publishing, Inc., P.O. Box 754, Huntsville, AR 72740, ATTN: Permissions Department.

Library of Congress Cataloging-in-Publication Data

Delcour-Min, Paulinne – 1948 -
Divine Fire by Paulinne Delcour-Min

Divine Fire offers a spellbinding trip to the future.

1. Spiritual   2. Past Lives   3. Future Lives   4. Metaphysical
I. Delcour-Min, Paulinne, 1948 - II. Metaphysical   III. Past Lives   IV. Title

Library of Congress Catalog Card Number: 2020940666
ISBN: 9781940265827

Cover Art and Layout: Victoria Cooper Art
Book set in: Multiple Fonts
Book Design: Tab Pillar
Published by:

OZARK
MOUNTAIN
PUBLISHING

PO Box 754, Huntsville, AR 72740
800-935-0045 or 479-738-2348; fax 479-738-2448
WWW.OZARKMT.COM

Printed in the United States of America

To Ye Min

You gave me the most precious of gifts—love, and my children.

The Book of the Future is for you and for them.

Rose, Clio, Jo, grandchild Eleanor, the future belongs to you

and to the brave souls who come after you. For sure, some of

us will be in that number, doing what has to be done.

That's why it's so important we get it right

now!

If you would prosper in challenging times,

this book is for you.

Making sense of the chaos in the world ...

Book 3

DIVINE FIRE:

The Keys to The Future

Books by Paulinne Delcour-Min

Spiritual Gold
Published by: Ozark Mountain Publishing

Holy Ice
Published by: Ozark mountain publishing

Divine Fire
Published by: Ozark Mountain Publishing

For more information about any of the above titles, soon to be released titles, or other items in our catalog, write, phone or visit our website:
Ozark Mountain Publishing, Inc.
PO Box 754, Huntsville, AR 72740
479-738-2348/800-935-0045
www.ozarkmt.com

Contents

Introduction

Divine Fire—a scary title for a book about the future, but blame my Higher Self for that!

I am a past life therapist who wanted to write a book, and one day in the autumn of 2007 my Higher Self dropped the title *Spiritual Gold, Holy Ice, Divine Fire* into my head. I was told what it was to be about and I knew many research sessions would be needed. The manuscript was submitted to Ozark Mountain Publishing in 2015, and in 2016 I heard back. I hadn't written a book—I'd written a trilogy! How my Higher Self must have laughed. Each part of the beautiful title had taken wing and flown off on its own.

Spiritual Gold's treasures provide the compass, *Holy Ice* unrolls a map of time and shares time's secrets, and *Divine Fire* provides keys to unlock the doors to the future and takes us through them.

We all need a compass, a map, and our keys.

But which door will we unlock?

If you have picked up this book today perhaps this is where you are meant to start—because the books link together in a circular fashion. Information flows through them and spirals around, taking you to ever higher levels of understanding. If you begin with *Divine Fire* the next book to read would be *Spiritual Gold*. You can hop onto the circle at any point and ride it round.

I love altered states of consciousness work. I love remembering my other lifetimes and learning from them, and I love helping others to realize there is so much more to life than what we can see and measure. I am not a hypnotherapist; I do my regression work in a more shamanic way, but I do love healing. And over the years I have found it possible to explore alternative time lines to free up an individual's future. If a decision they took in a past life had dire consequences, at the end of the regression session, after they've seen themselves pass through the threshold of death and understood the karma and lessons of their old life, it is possible to explore alternative choices and see where they lead.[1] When they find a more positive outcome it lifts them above their old karmic pattern and liberates their future. It can be the most healing thing to come out of the entire session and I call it doing "a new future." This is what I'm hoping my books will do for us—bring a little healing to our time line—tweak it in a positive direction and give us a new future.

This is a pivotal moment in our destiny.

A critical point in time.

Our future is hanging in the balance.

What you do, what you don't do, and even what you think could make the difference to how things turn out. By reading this book you will already have helped.

The seeds for this book were sown in 2007 when Veronica Fyland, my hypnotherapist friend, did the first sessions with me. In 2012 the seeds took root, and over the years the research has continued. When Veronica regresses me, I like to use the device of visualizing descending a staircase and entering a hallway of doors. One of the doors will attract me and I will open it and pass through, and step into another life. The story will unfold in response to her questions. When I am relaxed so deeply in the session that I can slip into this other life, it is like floating in a sea of knowledge. Passively floating. The questions hook the answers

1 Theoretical physics supports this; that each decision point generates a tear in space/time causing parallel worlds to bud off. The other realities are not flimsy wish fulfillment, you find cause and effect operates just as it does here. If someone is very entrenched in a negative pattern, say suicide, and have this theme running through several incarnations, then it can take multiple attempts with parallel realities before a more successful way of dealing with things is reached, when suicide is not seen as the go-to way out for difficult incarnations.

When doing this I ask people to go to an earlier time in that life, before the decision, and encourage them to listen to their dreams, heed their gut feelings or the whispers of their inner guides and their guardian angel—then they have another attempt when the choice point comes, and trace what happens from there, from important event to important event right to the end of the life. (It is interesting to note the different ages at which they die.)

out of that sea and pull the answers to me. I verbalize the answers and they are recorded on tape, and later the transcript of the tape provides the basis for a chapter.

The last five regressions were done with Ye Min, my husband, whom I have trained in my more shamanic way of working. We use a different journey into the inner world as you will see. Again, questions reveal the story, and healing happens before the return to ordinary reality.

Divine Fire is a document providing a record of our changing time line. Reading it again now, I was struck by the urgency and despair that tinged the earliest chapters. I have left the dates and events exactly as they came. If the projected dates seem too imminent or the events too drastic it is only because we have made great strides in changing the direction in which we were heading. I hope this is the case, because we were all set to sleepwalk off a cliff into extinction.

We have fallen asleep on our journey through matter, identified too closely with the material world. Lost in the dreams of matter we have forgotten who we truly are. That we are little droplets of the ocean of being that is the Creator, and as such we are eternal spiritual beings having an adventure exploring Creation. The adventure is hotting up at the moment as the environmental crisis unfolds all around us, and it may yet overwhelm us.

But we are not alone. We have help. At subliminal levels within our collective consciousness, at the back of our dreams, an alarm clock is ringing urging us to wake up. Because as the Native Americans say, this is

The Time of the Awakening.

If we can open our eyes we may step into the radiant dawn of a Golden Age—but if we don't, catastrophe looms. In the first chapter I will introduce you to the "alarm clock." It is a clock of many parts, and not all of them are on Earth.

There are three past lives in this book. The other research sessions brought up future lives and hidden events in this life relating to ET contact. The hidden events reveal other parts of our alarm clock.

- Chapter 1 -
Evolution, Devolution, Crystal Skulls, World Ages, and Agencies of Change!

Native American legends held in common by the Maya and Aztec descendants of Central America, by the Pueblo and Navajo Indians of the southwestern United States, right up to the Cherokee and Seneca Indians of the northeastern USA all tell of thirteen crystal skulls, the size of human skulls, which hold information vital for the very survival of the human race at a pivotal point in time. The legends say that though they've been scattered and hidden, one day the skulls will be brought back together to save us from disaster.

Well—we are at that point now!

After centuries of seclusion, ancient crystal skulls are being brought out into the world, because our future is in jeopardy. It's the skulls that are the bells on the "alarm clock" attempting to wake us up. The year 1998 saw the Wolf Song 1X World Peace Elders tour, where I met Mary Thunder and listened to indigenous elders from around the world when they visited England with their skulls. It was at the autumn equinox, and I had an unforgettable private sitting with the skull known as Sha Na Ra. There have been other tours and gatherings since, and on December 22 and 23, 2010, crystal skulls went to the UN.

Hunbatz Men, a Mayan Daykeeper, Don Pedro Chuc Pech, member of the Mayan Council of Elders, and Don Alejandro Cirilo Perez Oxlaj, Grand Elder of the living Maya, introduced them and presented them there. You can see it on YouTube.

Sha Na Ra, from Michele Nocerino

https://shanaracrystalskull.com/ (+1-925-577-3957)

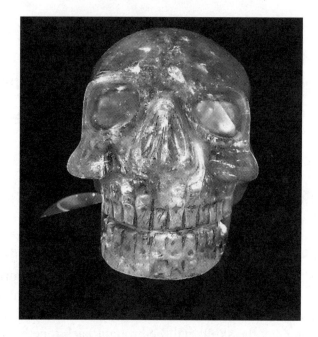

The Mitchell-Hedges Skull, by Bill Homann

http://mitchell-hedges.com/billhomann/ (+1-219-616-0886)

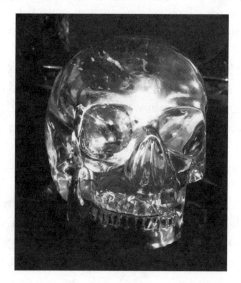

Evolution, Devolution, Crystal Skulls, World Ages, and Agencies of Change!

The Mitchell-Hedges Skull, by Ye Min

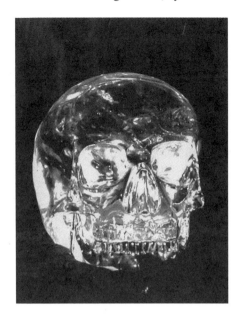

The Mitchell-Hedges Skull, by Bill Homann

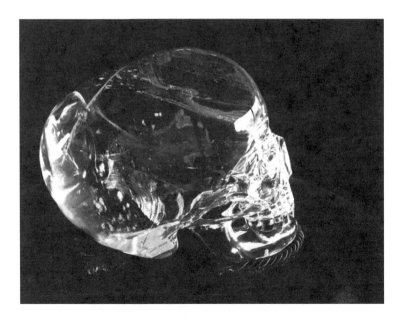

Divine Fire

The British Museum's Rock Crystal Skull
(and below the photo of me and the skull)

Photo gives an idea of size and a strange optical property of the skull

These ancient crystal skulls are multidimensional, and there is a subtle energy matrix connecting them with each other that resonates within our collective consciousness. Even modern skulls can interact with us in this way; their shape allows them to be like radio receivers and transmitters. They are tools, that are shaped like our seat of consciousness, and they are guardian forces, brought by the ancestors of their present-day guardians when they fled from an ancient homeland now lost beneath the sea.

They have been kept safe and handed down the generations.

The museums of the world hold a few, and they have attempted to determine the age of their skulls. But they cannot be carbon dated as quartz crystal holds no carbon. And though a skull's surface may tell of tool marks hinting at the time period of manufacture, as the British Museum confesses on its website, "There is no satisfactory scientific technique which can be used to accurately establish when a stone object was carved." This did not stop the museum from labeling their own skull (which they bought over 120 years ago) as "fake." They don't specify "fake" what, just show a photo of a tool mark. A scratched surface only proves that the surface has been scratched. It cannot tell us at what point in the existence of the object it was abraded and received the tool mark. Elsewhere they call it "probably fake" and hedge their bets.

Their skull is certainly not fake crystal. It is simply itself, a beautiful enigma that still functions as well as it ever did. Because that's the real question—do they work? They are tools to be used, not ornaments.

In the ancient world, crystal skulls were used as oracles and were cherished in temples, and this is where today's crystal-ball-fortune-telling tradition has its origins. The skulls are operated by thought. They resonate with our consciousness—treat them with respect and they may communicate with you via pictures seen inside their crystal, or by clairaudient experiences, where you hear them in your mind's ear. Ask a question, tune in, and you may be rewarded.

I was.

A picture in Sha Na Ra answered a personal question, and both the British Museum's skull and the Mitchell-Hedges skull have given me messages that appear in my books. Sha Na Ra has no trace of manufacture, nor has Max, who manifested in the earth and simply grew.[2] Were they gifts from another world? Some think so. Were skulls like Sha Na Ra worked on for generations and polished painstakingly with human hair? Perhaps. But it's not about when they were made that's important or even how they were made—it's do they work?

And they do work.

And they bring us a warning.

Because it depends on what we do now as to exactly which potential future will manifest for us on planet Earth: the good, the bad, or the shocking.

* * *

The universe unfolds at every moment. Things do not stand still for long, and change is constant. Worlds and beings evolve, or slip backward into the chaos of devolution. Entities are involved in these developments, and their interplay determines the fate of worlds. They are the forces in the archetypal battle between Light and Darkness, and these cosmic agencies include vast beings that barely have form.

2   Sha Na Ra was unearthed by "Nick" Nocerino in 1995 in Guererro province of Central Mexico.

The skull called Max, Crystallus Maximus, was discovered in 1924 in a tomb under a Mayan temple in Guatemala. Under microscopic examination Max appears to have formed naturally in the Earth. Dr. Robert Schoch of Boston University found Max to have formed from five separate crystals overlaid to form the skull. He said it cannot ever be reproduced because Max's structure consists of five separate crystalline matrixes that should not be mineralogically bonded together, but they are. With five such unique and succinct crystalline structures, differently aligned and each with a separate axis, Max could not have been carved even with today's sophisticated instruments and tools without fracturing the crystal formations that form him. His existence in mass is simply an enigma.

Max has a great ability to heal, and photos and information can be found at howtoraiseyourvibration. blogspot.com/2011/11/max-crystal-skull-also-called.html.

I recommend *The Mystery of the Crystal Skulls* by Chris Morton and Ceri Louise Thomas; there is much more about the legend and the skulls in their excellent book. It was from them I learned about the legend.

And it is always worth checking out www.crystalskulls.com for more information.

They exist in higher dimensions.

They are playing a grand cosmic game akin to chess, and when it comes to their game on Earth our authentic ancient crystal skulls are important pieces on their board. Chess requires one board, mapped out in squares of black and white—Darkness and Light—but this cosmic game is multilayered, stretching through many dimensions and involving at least three "boards" simultaneously. First there is the physical level of the game involving the solid 3D crystal skulls, which we can see, dotted about on the "chessboard" that is our Earth, then in the frequencies above that there is the etheric level of the game with its own set of skulls, and above that there is a level of light, set out with skulls of light. All the boards are connected, and the energies of primary cause flow down from one to the other until their effect is out-pictured by events happening in our 3D world.

So the game is multileveled, but it is also played on more than one world. It is being played throughout the universe. Worlds fall and worlds rise, and it is exciting for these beings to watch, as they manipulate the energy flows that lie behind change. We have our brief lives here, but these ancient beings experience time on a vast scale and see galaxies born and die. Their game is unfolding in our solar system, where there's an asteroid belt where a planet used to be, where ruined Mars struggles on, and Earth is poised on the brink of a critical and crucially decisive time.

Now more than ever we need our deepest wisdom to survive. And our ancient crystal skulls awaken that, they hold Earth's plan. Their higher dimensional skull-equivalents on the higher levels of the "game" interpenetrated the crystal lattice of the skull that we can see, and this is what gives the skulls their paranormal abilities.

They are lenses through which the energies of evolution are focused on our world.

They hold knowledge, and are gateways to more.

On February 9, 2008, when I was researching the crystal skulls for *Holy Ice* I visited the British Museum. From my past life memories, I know their skull as Ra Nan Sa. Ra summed up the cosmic battle between the forces of evolution and devolution being played out on planet Earth:

"It is foreseen since the dawn of time that this game will be played, that forces unbeknownst to your species, humankind, are at work shaping your destiny. Free will, yes, so you may yet lose the game if you all choose so, but with the loving heart that is so large and so open with your species you can win spectacularly. And so it has been seen since the beginnings of time for your world. Be cheerful and of good heart for things unfold as they are destined to do."

The Big Bang launched Creation, and Creation's purpose was to be a grand game for the Creator to behold. What makes the game exciting is the battle between Light and Darkness. That is why we have duality. It is where the fruits of Creation form. Throughout the cosmos the battle rages on, while on Earth the next moves in the game are about to be made ... as we walk between two worlds with our future in flux.

We live in extraordinary times. The year 2012 captured the imagination of people all over the world because the winter solstice marked the end of a great cycle of time—and some thought it might mark the end of considerably more than that! Speculation escalated, fueled by ancient prophecies and the Mayan calendar, and 2012 became a powerful and iconic date that resounded in the psyches of many people around the globe. The world woke up, there was the blockbuster movie *2012,* and a great many books. One example was *Beyond 2012: Catastrophe or Ecstasy* by Geoff Stray, and the title neatly sums up the poles our future is fluxing between.

The facts are this: according to the Maya there have been three previous world ages before ours, each one lasting 5,125 years and each one ending in devastation. The third age ended on August 13, 3114 BC, as Atlantis sank beneath the waves in a catastrophic event. The ancestors of the Maya fled from this destruction and guarded their knowledge of calendrics and time, and since then they have marked down the days with their Long Count calendar. The Long Count tells us we are now poised between the end of the fourth world age and the beginning of a fifth. As we go about our lives today we are literally walking between the two worlds, the fourth and the fifth.

There are those who disputed the end date, suggesting a few years ahead, but I was grateful for the hype 2012 attracted because it was the spur to look and see what exactly *was* lying ahead at this important time. Now, the big difference between the past and the future is that the past is solid compared with the ever-mutating possibilities of the future. Certain decisions bring about certain possibilities, and we are constantly weaving the cloth from which our future will be cut. Our consciousness can enter the parallel realities of the future, but the one we will finally access depends on choices we are yet to make.

I think we can understand how this can be—especially in relation to the future—but it is also true that parallel realities exist in the present moment. Quantum physics shows us that subatomic particles tend to slip in and out of parallel worlds, and there are regressionists like Dick Sutphen who have explored in depth the possibility that we, too, may have parallel existences of which we are not consciously aware. It is as if our spirit, our particular droplet of the Divine's ocean of being, is powerful enough to sustain several points of embodied consciousness at the same time, all feeding their experiences into the soul memory bank. Some consciousness is housed in molecular bodies—solid physical bodies like ours, while other expressions of our soul may be encased in nonmolecular bodies of force or energy or thought. And if we access such parallel lives we find hidden and surprising things. The parallels can be searched for intentionally, but sometimes they just pop up in the normal course of regression because the answer being looked for lies there. This has happened to me and it happened again at the very start of the research for *Divine Fire*.

By the end of the first set of regressions all three aspects of time—the past, the present, and the future—had contributed their secrets for the book. The chapters are presented in the order in which the information came, and they begin with a transcript of the session from a present parallel existence of mine.

The next moves are about to be made in the great cosmic battle of Evolution v. Devolution on planet Earth ... and I was about to stumble upon:

"Forces unbeknownst to your species (that) are at work shaping your destiny."

In other words, agencies of change!

- Chapter 2 -
AD 2012–2048: The Time of Purification

Veronica Fyland, my hypnotherapist friend, has been on the adventure with me from the start of the research for the books. We work well together, Veronica and I, and it was time to do the first session for *Divine Fire*.

I have a therapy room at my home where I work, and the process was about to begin. I lay on my couch, feeling relaxed, with my eyes closed.

Veronica began the induction. The induction is designed to help me focus within, to loosen my consciousness from the constraints of the outer world, and this is how I change my relationship with time. Soft music plays in the background while I concentrate on Veronica's voice and follow her instructions. When she thinks I am ready she asks me to visualize a staircase.

I see one clearly in my mind's eye and am directed to descend, step by step.

This symbolizes changing my level of consciousness.

We never know what a session will bring and this time the staircase gives out onto a circular space illumined by a peachy-gold glow. Here I feel uplifted, serene, and peaceful. I bask in the warm, loving light.

But then I notice that incongruously right in the center of this spiritual place sits a jumble of objects. My subconscious, in cahoots with my Higher Self, has placed a pile of clutter there for me to find—and the unexpected jumble of stuff makes me laugh! With this I've gone from the sublime to the ridiculous. It's a mad mix. There's a hold-all bag containing scrolls; bits of old tools and a few golden things; and a futuristic orange duffle bag from which protrudes a violet tube.

Veronica directs me to see if there is a special being of knowledge and wisdom who can help me understand this and guide me through the session. My thoughts go to Hera, and she appears beside me, tall and semitransparent, willowy and graceful.[3] She pulls the largest scroll out of the hold-all and begins unrolling it. I can't understand the pictures or read the script on the scroll, although it is written quite distinctly in black. I do not recognize the language at all, and so I ask her what it is about. All she will say is, "You will remember."

But before I can do that I have to go further on the journey into the inner world; I need to find the doors to my memories, and only then will I understand the significance of the objects. Hera puts her hand on my waist and ushers me into the corridor where the doors are to be found.

The door I'm drawn to this time is high-gloss orange—the same color as the bag with the tube. There is a golden doorknob surrounded by intricate gold tracery, I wonder if a script is disguised in the patterning? … I feel it might tell a story of its own … and maybe I will be able to make sense of it on my return.

Before I open the door Hera places a protective hooded cloak about my shoulders. This is an "energy field to keep me safe," and although it looks transparent it is scattered over with sparkles reminiscent of constellations of stars. Hera confirms I am about to see a life important for the book—and in particular very important for the years after 2012. All I'm told is, "You will understand when you see it."

I put my hand on the golden knob, open the door, and visualize myself stepping through. First there's a glimpse of green grass in a field, and then feelings of confusion, something violet flashes past me and I find myself floating in space.

Around me everything is black.

But … there are stars.

---

3 Since my school days my main inner (spirit) guide had been Francis, who was my abbot in a monastic life in eleventh-century England, but since working on the crystal skulls' material Hera has come to help.

Veronica directs me to become aware of myself, and she asks me to describe myself.

I know I am in the vastness of the universe.

This is where I live, and I live here in joyous freedom. I know I have fun riding on the currents of the universe, gliding on galactic tides, and when I look more closely at my body I find it consists purely of energy. It appears white to me—but I am not human. Nor am I alone. I am with others of my kind, and this is a very different consciousness to my "Paulinne" self.

Communication flows in response to Veronica's questioning.

Pegasus the Winged Horse

South of the equator Pegasus looks like this, but in northern skies
the constellation of stars we know as Pegasus is upside down, and
looks like the star map below.

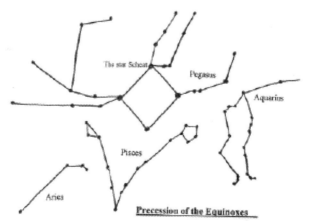

Precession of the Equinoxes

The Age of Aries was followed by the Age of Pisces, and we are slowly moving
into the Age of Aquarius now. But notice Pegasus's position – Pegasus is bridging
the gap between Pisces and Aquarius.

We know the ancient seers of Earth saw us when they meditated in their temples and were deep in their inner-world processes. When they sought to know God and expanded their awareness outward into the universe they glimpsed us, with our white wings unfurled, as we glided on the currents of the stars, as the eagles of Earth ride on the currents of the air. Their legends speak of Pegasus, the winged horse.

But we are many, and like the wild horses of Earth we travel together in herds. And like them we have our territories, which we circle on our migrations through the universe, but we are not of dense matter as are they. Our energy bodies are nearer to the divine frequencies, and so we are invisible to the eyes of matter however hard they look, be they human or machine eyes.

There are many herds like ours.

We fly with manes streaming out like sun-fire, and it is from the suns that we get our energy. The sun and the stars in your sky are the physical manifestations of the higher energy of God-force that is focused at those points in the universe. The suns beam out that energy and bring life to the worlds, and we are agents of the suns, forces to bring harmony and stamp out disharmony.

Our communication is with thought.

Oh, yes, we have names, as the dolphins in your seas have names for each other. We know who we are, and I am Ahwoooooooh.

We graze on the starlight of a million suns as we fly in joyous freedom, soaring between worlds and riding star currents from sun to sun. We are far too big to actually alight on a world, but we feel their energies as we pass by. Some feel good to us and others repel us—their disharmony feels irritating to us. If we find a world very irritating we trample it. Irritation occurs where beings have lost their harmony, and where the energy emanations of their world are affecting other worlds. When this happens we gather round, circling the world, and we attack it with our focused mental powers; we trample it with wave after wave of energy, targeting the beings that are causing the problem. We could scorch them out. We could alter the frequency of their world so they could no longer hold there, or we could alter the frequency of their cells so they more readily destruct and create cancers. We could manipulate viruses and immune systems. Oh, there is so much we can do. But in very extreme cases we exterminate the world also. Sometimes the beings have subverted the world's spirit, or in certain sinister cases the beings were more of a direct expression of the planet's spirit that had turned negative.

It is true to say we've seen all sorts of things as we've gone through the universe, but as long as a world is innocent we wouldn't trample it, whatever fate we had to mete out to the beings there. And mostly the Creator's plan is unfolding beautifully—but sometimes not.

We are passing by the outer planets of your solar system now [this was back in 2008] on our way to see Sol. We've been there many times before, and Sol is a point of reference for us on our endless circuit. It's a battered old system this, with asteroids where there should be a world, but there's work to be done, and we've been called.

We're always traveling, but we travel with a purpose. We oversee the unfoldment of Creation, like gardeners weed a garden, sorting out problems that arise, and this is part of the area we protect. We survey it and check up on it, and we bring change if it is needed. We know that Mars has its problems. It is a damaged world, but not a dead one nor an empty one, but it is Earth that concerns us now.

The Earth spirit has been calling for help, and we're answering that call.

Change is needed and we will bring it.

Usually we just get rid of the problem, and the problem on Earth is humankind. They are acting like planetary lice, like an uncontrolled cancerous parasite. Greed and exploitation are causing pollution affecting the atmosphere and the seas and the physical fabric of the world. Humans are having a negative impact on other life forms, there's too many of them and they're not acting responsibly and sharing.

We've had to do this before, I know.

We had to send them back to the caves. We've had to do all sorts before. I think they'll eventually get it right, but now we're on our way to sort them out again.

The sun isn't happy about Earth.

It's been beaming out energy to Earth in the solar flares, so that the spiritual force that lies behind the solar activity can bring change. But they're very resistant on Earth, always devising ways to get round it instead of gracefully flowing and evolving with the changes. They're too clever by half and very resistant. The God-force has sent them many spiritual teachers down the ages, and although they were listened to, they never really had the lasting impact that they should have had. God has been trying to talk to his children through the avatars and the prophets, but there comes a time when there has to be a trampling so new shoots can grow, and that's what we're on our way to do ...

You could say humankind has brought this on itself as a collective whole. Not everyone has caused the problem and not everyone will get trampled, because it isn't the Creator's will that humankind should disappear, but it needs a huge shake-up and certain low elements need to be culled.

Humankind has been given very big heart centers, and they have to learn to live through their hearts, and those that don't ... well, there's not really any place for them. Their crown chakras should be open to God, so that God's energy can flow down into them to help them evolve, but so many have managed to close their crowns that God has been unable to talk to his children. And because their crown chakras are so closed, their energies short circuit and they feel lost and lonely and empty, and they try to get more and more money. But it never fills the emptiness inside them, because no matter how much they have, they feel they never have enough, and it's all because they've cut themselves off from the source of the only sustenance that they really need.

Humankind will have to change. They can't go on causing pain to their world and to the other creatures who share it with them; and to the angels who watch; and to the sun that has to listen to Earth's screams; and pain to the other worlds that hear about it as the sun beams it out with the photons of light that are constantly showering out into the universe.

It's not a secret.

There are many eyes watching Earth now, and many beings trying to help them change. Many beings from many worlds—who have all been through the process of the trampling themselves—are there now trying to help them. They have incarnated into the species bringing their subliminal memories of past catastrophes with them to try and avert what might be coming. There's a tremendous focus of interest to try to change the situation and turn it around. But if all else fails there will be a trampling, because it simply can't go on.

We shall be with you by the end of 2012, and we shall stay until we are done with you in 2048.

We're not cruel; we're just agencies for change.

We get told there's a problem and that there needs to be a shift, and so we're the agencies that bring about that shift so the Creator's plan can unfold. And the problem concerns oil, pollution, money, war, poverty, and prisons, the lack of beauty in education, the lack of skills for all the important things like spiritual development. The people are being starved of all the things they should really have because money, oil, and greed have become the gods. A very few hold most of the money, yet they enslave the masses, so although the people may have good hearts they have been rendered powerless. They need to take back their power, not in a bad way, but they need to wake up out of that dream of madness and start being accountable for their own actions and their own hearts and then there would be a change.

There are other things for us to deal with before Earth, but we're on our way. Take heed before it's too late, because the storm is gathering. Change is coming, be prepared. You won't see us but we will be there.

Now this session was conducted in the summer of 2008, and four long years would have to elapse before the Pegasus beings swept in, like the biblical four horsemen of the apocalypse, bringing famine, pestilence, war, and death.[4]

So with 2012 well behind us now, we are living through the years of the Pegasus purge, and the challenge this brings is for us to increase our harmony. We need to live in harmony with our world, with ourselves, and with each other. Harmony is our

4 Found in the Holy Bible, Revelation chapter 6:1–8, where white, red, black, and pale horses are harbingers of the Last Judgment and set a divine apocalypse upon the world. Written two thousand years ago it was a prophecy of future tribulations in which many will die. It was only later I connected this with Pegasus, but it does sound spookily similar—like the Pegasus beings are the horses of the apocalypse, the bringers of famine, pestilence, war, and death.

best protection from the chaos Pegasus causes, and our personal harmony always lies within our own power. Try not to let people or events steal it from you.

There are always ways to restore it, and one is through doing things we enjoy, however simple—like stroking a pet, walking in nature or in our local park, gardening, meditating, using music, color, scent, beauty, literature or at the very least by focusing on our breath—slowing it down and counting silently as we inhale and exhale. One way to be in the world but not of it is to become aware of the point of golden light in your abdomen that lies just below your navel, and to let that grow until its radiance buffers you from whatever unhappiness is going on around you; by doing this you are tuning in to a higher dimension and tuning out of this level of reality a little, literally raising your vibrations. And flower remedies can really help here too. The Doctor Bach "Rescue Remedy" is a combination of five flower essences preserved in brandy—and a few drops provide instant lift to soothe upsets and restore balance. The harmony of the flowers helps to restore your harmony. A little sunshine does us good too; it strengthens your aura and brings a feeling of well-being, as it nourishes you on many levels.

But no matter how harmonious we are, our lives will still be influenced by our karma and so some events are inevitable. However, if we listen to our intuition (inner-tuition) our guides and angels can help us. Heed your dreams and have the courage to follow inner promptings, and your intuition will help you to be in the right place at the right time. And remember, Pegasus affects us *all*, so those whose disharmonious agendas are greed and exploitation will have more reason to fear the trampling than most. All the money in the world is not going to hide anyone from the Pegasus purge in the years of purification. The shadowy elite with their associated entities have more reason to fear Pegasus than the rest of us do.

The crystal skulls are forces that restore harmony and that is how they bring about healing, and perhaps it is no accident that at the present time there is more interest in them than ever before.

(But were they to be stolen it would not profit the thieves. They would find themselves amplified into even bigger targets. Skulls with wrongful guardians earn a reputation for being cursed. It is said that's how the Smithsonian got their skull, sent in by a donor who committed suicide after a string of misfortunes, and though sent anonymously he was traced through a solicitor.)

At the end of the session, as I came back through the door I examined the tracery around the golden doorknob. Mixed in with moons and stars were the words *"Take heed before it is too late, there is a gathering storm, the clouds are coming."* And before we finished the session I accessed a hidden message that had been given to me a few days earlier, at my second audience with Ra Nan Sa on July 27, 2008. It ran:

For it is time now for man to be counted, to be accountable for his actions and choices, not to be the slave of any master but to stand alone and for himself and for what he believes in. The time is coming that change can not be denied, and the outcome is as yet uncertain.

There is still time to change. The choice is yours but you must make it, or it will be made for you by those who think they are your masters, those inspired by the forces of greed and by the status quo, and by the power of money and oil, and all those commodities which are deemed to be more vital than life itself in certain quarters.

The time of choice is at hand. You alone answer the Creator at the end of your life and He will be listening very carefully for the answers you give Him about the choices that you made. Choose wisely, my children, there is much help available to you. You have the written words of the prophets, the religious teachers down the ages. You have your own hearts, you have your prayers to God. You have much help, use it. Do not forfeit the choice or have it taken from you, made by others because you couldn't be bothered. Think about your actions, your thoughts. Think about the consequences to your generation and the generations that follow. Leave a world for your children and grandchildren and great-grandchildren, or that world may be taken from you. The choice is yours. Make it wisely.

Our world is poised on the threshold of a fundamental change. Whether this is for better or for worse depends on what we do. We can increase our efforts to be ecologically responsible and less polluting, but I also believe we will influence what will happen by the state of our collective consciousness. If we can lighten our hearts and minds we will experience an increase in our inner harmony and personal radiance, and as we transform we will begin to express more of our true divine nature. Heavy emotions like bitterness and resentment, lack of forgiveness, the darkness of fears, or the consuming fires of anger all destroy our harmony, and such emotional baggage weighs us down. If we can count our blessings and focus on thoughts of joy and love, and try to laugh in the face of trials and difficulties, we can begin to shed the old way of being in the world like a snake sheds a skin it has outgrown. This increased harmony will be our greatest protection and a gift to help heal our world. Consider your own thoughts and actions and then ask yourself, "What is this doing to my radiance? How is this affecting my harmony?" If it is enhancing it, continue. If it is diminishing it, let it go.

We can only change ourselves,
but by doing that we change the world.

Together we could create heaven on Earth.
The alternative is hell on Earth.
We choose.

* * *

Prophecies

As time went on I came across various things that tied in with the predicted time of purging.

While checking out Native American prophecies I found that the Hopi speak of "**the time of purification**," and that a great many of their other prophecies have already been fulfilled.[5] Among Native Americans the Hopi are known as "the wisdom keepers" and the Maya are "the keepers of time" because of their elaborate system of calendars which enable them to track the ages. In *The Mystery of the Crystal Skulls* Mayan priest/shaman Don Alejandro Cirilo Oxlaj Peres, president of the National Council of Elders, Mayas, Xinca, and Garifuna as he was then, the same Don Alejandro who took crystal skulls to the UN in 2010, is reported as saying:

"Now is the time of the awakening. This is your job now to awaken. The Vale of the Nine Hells is past and the Time of Warning has now arrived. It is time to prepare for the Age of the Thirteen Heavens ... The time approaches when you will be required to love all things, to love a world that has gone crazy, to rebalance the heavens and the Earth."

"The thirteen Heavens will begin after sunset on 21 December in the year 2012. The next day after that is written in our Long Count calendar as 13.0.0.0.0. This number in our sacred calendar represents a new form of government, a new way of understanding each other so that we will no longer see each other with indifference and mistreat each other on this Earth. This date represents the start of the Thirteen Heavens. The date when the new world will begin. This will be the start of a new 13 Baktun period. This is what is written in the book of Chilam Balam. And, as prophesied, the skulls are returning for the Time of Warning as the great legend said, because now is the time that what was written must be fulfilled.

5 Hopi Prophecies—Prophecy Rock—Crystalinks at https://www.crystalinks.com > hopi2 is a site with a lot of information. (23.8.2019) Scroll down a fair way to find: "This is the First Sign" and read on to the Ninth Sign.

And so the Council of Elders is now meeting, guided by the prophecies and by the wisdom of the skulls, because now is the time to awaken the world ... for now the Time of the Awakening is upon us. The skulls are now here to awaken our consciousness, to help us learn to love all things. It is written in the calendar that the world will listen now, that the world will now hear the heartbeat of Mother Earth." [6]

According to Don Alejandro, the Nine Hells ended and the Time of Warning began as the 16th of August became the 17th of August in 1987, and this was celebrated as the Harmonic Convergence by many around the world. At that time I wasn't aware of the skulls, or of Don Alejandro, although I would meet him ten years later. No, I heard about this via the work of Jose Arguelles.

That night my friends and I kept a vigil on Alderley Edge, a local vantage point south of Manchester, England, where I lived at the time. Its sandstone cliffs were first mined for copper in the early Bronze Age and it is a place of history and legend. There is said to be a cave beneath it, guarded by an old wizard and filled with knights in armor and their milk-white horses, all sleeping an enchanted sleep, ready for their country's hour of need when they will awaken and fight a great battle on the plain below.

That dawn, when the sun rose over the plain in front of us, it really was as if the world was being made new by golden light. We visualized the light flowing along energy pathways and going all over the world, as Jose had suggested. It was magical. So magical that everyone wanted to go again the following year, and so we did, and by then I had met my husband, Ye. It was nice, but it was just a normal dawn and we didn't bother again after that. But of course Alderley Edge had been my first choice as the place of power to see in the winter solstice for 2012.

---

6 *The Mystery of the Crystal Skulls,* pages 343, 344, and 349.

AD 2012–2048: The Time of Purification

Winter Solstice 2012

Tynemouth

by the North Sea

But time had moved on. December weather was a far cry from a balmy August star-strewn night, and I was no longer living in Manchester. So when the time came it wasn't to Alderley Edge that Ye and I were driving in the freezing December darkness, but to a headland at the mouth of the river Tyne, south of Whitley Bay, on England's northeast coast. There had been days of dreadful weather. Dark days, with the sky thickly shrouded in cloud, but the rain had stopped at last and by a ruined old castle and ancient priory, battered by the wind, we stood staring eastward out over the North Sea, as we waited for the dawn.

I thought about what I had been told.

"You are a child of the stars and a daughter of the ancient world. You link the two ages and will stitch them together with your staff. You are part of a family of way-showers, part of a global shamanic assistance, working together in unknowing harmony."

I certainly wanted to greet the Pegasus beings because they were bringing our future;[7] I wanted to honor both Poseidon and his queen, because we definitely didn't need a repeat of the Atlantean catastrophe; and I wanted to balance the heavens and the Earth, as was done in lives past. So with my crystal moon fan I swept away the moon, with my crystal sun fan I swept a path for the sun to arise anew. We blew conch shells to greet and to honor, and with the Earth healing staff I had been inspired to make many years before I symbolically called forth the balance. And in the wind and the freshness of that rain-cleansed morning the sun rose and the sky filled with the light of the new sun.[8]

---

7 By this time I'd completed the initial research for *Divine Fire*; I'd looked ahead and seen what the alternative was if they didn't come.

8 A solstice is a three-day event. The cloud cover was so very thick and the weather so bad that disappointingly we had to wait until the third day, Sunday, the 23rd of December, before it felt right—and before there was any chance of a visible dawn to celebrate. (We were to learn later in a newsletter from the crystal skull website www.crystalskulls.com, that the Hopi had said the sky was not right on the 21st, and that in Hopiland they too had waited until the 23rd.) *"The clouds are coming"* had been written on the door to the session, but I wasn't expecting this to be quite so literally the case!

The conch shells we found in Glastonbury that July. Ye plays the saxophone so he can coax amazing sounds out of these shell trumpets, and he managed to teach me to play them a little. My staff has a serpent coiling up it, with gourds at the top filled with crystals to make sound chambers. It is tipped with an amethyst (to transmute), and it is decorated with stars (for the heavens), shells (for the seas), and spirals to denote the energies inherent in the sacred places of our lands. Since the solstice I have felt lighter and freer. I feel like I'm living in my time at last, the time I have

But to return to Pegasus in the light of the words of Don Alejandro: Pegasus is with us now as we enter the Thirteen Heavens. The stamping out and trampling of disharmony is what will plunge us into "a world that has gone crazy" but this is the threshold to the Heavens. To enter a dwelling we first wipe our feet on the doormat to brush off unwanted things we may have brought with us, and so as we cross the threshold of the Thirteen Heavens Pegasus will shake from us the things we need to leave behind before we can enter the new state of being.

The name Pegasus comes down to us from ancient Greece. The Greek legends say Pegasus's father was Poseidon and his mother was the Gorgon, Medusa. So in terms of what the myths of the classical world tell us about him, from his father he inherits a god's spiritual power and the power to shake things up—in the way storms and earthquakes do—and from his mother he inherits rage and the power to transform. Snake-haired Medusa turned those who looked at her to stone.

Bearing in mind how instrumental Poseidon was to the events at the end of the last world age, when Atlantis was destroyed by water,[9] it is interesting to see one of his sons strategically positioned at the end of this one. And this is literally the case if you consider the starry constellations in the night sky.

When the Pegasus material came up in the session I did not connect it with the constellation; I could not even have told you where those stars were in the night sky. But while I was editing this chapter I found that the constellation of stars called "Pegasus" lies between the constellations of Pisces and Aquarius. The upper body of the horse is formed by a square of four stars to be found toward the end of Pisces, and the stars of his outstretched neck form a bridge between Pisces and Aquarius. (In the northern

---

come here for.

Merlin was the name of the guide who came into my meditation when I was asking for advice on how to best greet the dawn. He was most helpful, and he said he had a role to play, "Shepherding the energies of place on the other levels." Strangely enough Merlin is the wizard associated with Alderley Edge. (I hadn't asked for Merlin—just for the highest appropriate guide—and I had not met him in meditation before. Although I would later, and I would find a very close connection with him through a past life I looked at in 2019 that I was able to include in *Holy Ice* before it went to press.)

9 The story of the end of Atlantis is in *Holy Ice*.

hemisphere Pegasus appears upside down, while viewed from the southern hemisphere he is the right way up.)

In terms of the calendar of the zodiac we are moving out of the Age of Pisces and entering into the Age of Aquarius. It is a strange coincidence that the constellation of Pegasus marks the gateway in time and space where the energies of the Pegasus purge will come pouring through. The ancient seers gave these stars their name, and I don't think it was an accident.

The zodiac is very old. It comes to us from ancient Babylonia. Thousands of years ago when Babylonian astronomers looked at the night sky they were using the same system of star groupings that our astronomers still use today. This knowledge passed down the ages to us and traveled from country to country. The ancient Egyptians carved a bas-relief of a huge zodiac on the ceiling of the temple of Hathor and Isis at Denderah in Egypt. The original is now in the Louvre museum in Paris while a replica takes its place in the temple, but what is important about the carving is that it shows almost 26,000 years of time laid out in a great circular calendar of the heavens. It shows the precession of the equinoxes,[10] and carved between Pisces and Aquarius is a mysterious feature. The square of Pegasus (as the four stars that make up his body are known) carries within it what has been referred to as "the tablet of destiny." Carved into the stone is what looks like a tablet covered in lines of script; and one way to interpret it is that just as the Ten Commandments were written down on tablets of stone, so humankind's destiny is written down and held within Pegasus … that Pegasus shaking us up and influencing us is ordained—a sort of cosmic check and balance. (The extent of the shaking will be determined by how much shaking we need before we're restored

10 A zodiacal age lasts approximately 2,160 years, although they vary a little. Every 2,160 years the zodiacal constellation in the predawn eastern sky slowly changes, moving from one to the next as we move backward through the twelve constellations of the zodiac. This effect happens because of the tilt in the Earth's axis as we move through space, and it is called the precession of the equinoxes.

It takes almost 26,000 years for the Earth to complete her orbit through the twelve constellations of the zodiac, and by a strange coincidence the Mayan Great Year lasts the same length of time. The Maya divide the Great Year into five world ages, each lasting 5,125 years. The fifth world age, beginning with the Thirteen Heavens, will complete their Great Year.

Babylon is in modern-day Iraq while the lands of the Maya lie on the other side of the world—so what chance then that they should both use 26,000 years as a complete cycle?

to balance.)

The carving is conservatively dated to 50 BC but some think it considerably older, and certainly the knowledge it contains is ancient Babylonian star lore that had found its way to Egypt.

Whether you believe in astrology or not it is remarkable that astrology tells us that the influence of Pegasus causes extreme misfortune, but that for those open to its higher manifestation there is a positive influence of creativity. Astrology's advice is to be open to the higher!

To quote an astrologer:

Pegasus was born from the union of Neptune [as the Romans called Poseidon] and Medusa. In the astrological influence of this constellation we can see the themes of the sea and spirituality from Neptune, and the rage from Medusa. The story of Pegasus fits well as the constellation of this age. Global warming, sea level rise, increased frequency and intensity of storms. "Only for some" can the higher manifestation of this star [Scheat[11]] be perceived. The majority of humanity are scared of these changes or ignore them as if they are not happening.

Pegasus is carrying us from the Ages of Pisces to Aquarius as the changes in our environment continue to escalate, and as the effect on the collective consciousness deepens, it will be up to the minority of people in tune with the spiritual side to help the rest of humanity through this difficult time. Astrologers, intuitive healers and all associated new-agers and freaks are becoming increasingly important and useful as the old security gives way to Uranian times.

Pegasus stretches across the constellations of Pisces and Aquarius, so represents evolution between one mode of thinking to another. ... Pegasus representing the shift in mindset from

---

11 Scheat is the second brightest star in the square of Pegasus, the name means "**who goeth and returneth.**" (Very apt for a herd of Pegasus beings patroling our bit of the galaxy on an endless circuit.) It is a fixed star, a red giant with a total luminosity of 1500 times that of our sun. We are under the influence of Scheat right now (and will be to the end of the century), because "when a fixed star moves via the precession of the equinoxes to zero degrees Aries, it is called the 'Star of the Age.' The last one and the next one are both in Pegasus, giving weight to Pegasus being the constellation of this age." From Astrologyking.com (9.4.2014).

worshipping a God to becoming your own God. But when one looks at the stars in Pegasus, it is evident the transition is not going to be easy.[12]

Chief among Pegasus's stars is Scheat, chillingly described elsewhere as, "A terrible scorpionic star with terminative yet transforming potencies."[13]

Pegasus was born in violent circumstances. Poseidon had raped Medusa, Perseus the Greek hero had cut off her head, and Pegasus was born from the blood that dripped from it into the sea. But from these shocking and violent images sprang the innocence and beauty of the white winged horse—a horse who flew to the home of the gods, and was entrusted by Zeus to carry his divine thunderbolts. According to the Greek myths when Pegasus was rewarded for his service by being transformed into a constellation of stars, one pure white wing feather drifted down to the Earth.

Out of the bloodshed and trauma came transcendence.

And that's what will happen again.

It really fits with my findings.

And it explains the purpose of this book, because it is to help people open to the higher, to the spiritual side of things—because that's the only way to ride out the Pegasus purge and transcend. But the astrologers and I both came by our knowledge through totally different routes. I thought this was amazing.

* * *

Before I did this session my only connection with Pegasus was as a power animal. Years before he had popped up in a soul therapy session in response to the question, "Is there a power animal you need to be connected to?" and "abuse of power" was a negative aspect that had had to be released before this was done—because my Pegasus had destroyed a world. I saw it quite clearly: it exploded. It had really annoyed him and he had targeted it with thought. (It was a puzzle to me at the time but now I can

12 Astrologyking.com (9.4.2014).
13 www.astronova.nu/pegasus1.html (10.4.2014).

understand it.)

Pegasus's gift is **power**.

If we can ride him we will soar through the years of change.

I had often wondered how we got our power animals, and there may be various routes by which they come to us, but one way is for us to have lived as one of them. And in that way we acquire their qualities which become our gifts; and this is certainly the case with old Peg. While I am here on Earth, part of my soul essence is still out there stampeding through the universe and trampling irritating worlds!

And quite possibly, in fact almost certainly, so is yours …

- Chapter 3 -
Spiritual Alchemy

This chapter of *Divine Fire* dips back into the past. This is where the golden threads of time tie up in the search for eternal truth—in other words where the ancient world meets up with the beginnings of the modern. So hang on to your hat—we're off to eighteenth-century France! That's before the French Revolution.

Now the city of Montpellier in the south of France was old, even in the eighteenth century, which is when the events in this chapter took place. King Louis XV was on the throne, it was the Age of Reason, men wore powdered wigs, women wore extravagant brocade dresses, and fashionable furniture was ridiculously fancy. Aristocrats, like the family in this life story, lived lives of ease, while it was a very different tale for the poor. However, just because you were rich does not mean everything went your way... especially not if you were a threat to an already beleaguered Catholic Church, whose grip on people's minds had been slipping ever since the Age of Reason began. No, you crossed the Church at your peril, as somebody found out.

Montpellier is famous for two things: its university and its castle. The university had been founded as long ago as AD 1160, and its castle was even older. The university attracted free thinkers, whose ideas sometimes caused trouble ... and the feudal lords in the castle ruthlessly wielded their power with impunity, and interpreted the laws of the land to suit themselves. The feudal lords got away with many things because the castle's dungeons were big enough to hold their secrets, and the dead don't talk.

Over time the secrets became a powerful force.

Relentlessly they drew people to them.

They drew me.

Veronica and I never knew where a session would take us, but this one was a surprise.

Secrets, Treasure, and Eternal Truth

I open the door to my memories … and stepped through into a dark, dank place. It stank of rancid cellars and I soon realized I was in a dungeon. I tried not to breathe, but it was impossible to avoid inhaling the stench of ancient damp and decaying bones. The clammy air pressed itself around me as though Death himself was breathing on my skin.

I felt sick and wished I hadn't come.

I was now Agatha.

Agatha de Cressy, a French noblewoman.

And as I gingerly walked forward into the fetid gloom an unseen cobweb brushed my cheek. I couldn't have been more shocked if it had been Death's fingernail tracing his mark upon my face.

I had to force myself to go on.

The jailor was ahead of me and I didn't want to be alone.

As we moved through the darkness our lanterns spilled light, revealing a succession of small cells to our left and to our right— each built with gates made stoutly of iron bars. People had been left here to die, over the centuries, just left here to rot where they fell. My lantern's light glanced off the dust and bones they'd left behind, which was all that gave testament to the fact that the poor souls had ever lived at all. I knew there'd be no tombstones for them to mark their passing from life … and I clutched my cloak tighter about me.

Cobwebs and filth lay over everything.

I thanked God for the bonnet that was shielding my hair; I couldn't help but feel sullied by the place. My fashionable shoes and dainty footsteps were no match for the jailer's stride and I was falling farther behind him. His words drifted to me through the echoing gloom and I could hear him muttering, "'Tis no place fer a lady."

He had unlocked one of the iron gates to the left by the time I caught up with him, and he was holding his lantern on high, revealing the small chamber and its contents for my inspection.

"'Ere's what yer want, missy," he said, pointing to a pitiful heap of rags and bones on the floor.

Then he set about, cheerily sweeping them up and shoveling them into the sack we had with us for the purpose.

I watched as he worked.

I felt weighed down by the despair of the place, and by the depth of a recent sadness I carried. My favorite granddad, the one on my mother's side of the family, had died, and I was still in mourning for him.

He had been dear to me, my granddad, and since his death I had suffered a succession of bad dreams. Wherever he was now, he was troubled—and he'd been disturbing my sleep by coming to me in dreams and telling me I had to finish something for him. It appeared he'd left unfinished business behind him when he died, and his spirit could find no rest.

At first I'd hoped it would all just go away, that the dreams would stop. But alas, they hadn't, and as time went by they got worse. I'd come to this place of desolation hoping to put an end to my nightmares, hoping to restore my sleep. I was here to collect the bones of an ancestor and to find the key to a very valuable lost treasure.

The bones were those of my grandfather's father, my great-grandfather.

I knew that he had angered the Church *and* the feudal lord at the castle, and it was said he possessed a great treasure. Great-grandfather Guillaume had been tried for heresy, treason, this, that, or the other, and had been found guilty. He had been locked away here in squalor and gloom over what our family had always regarded as trumped-up charges. His enemies had left him to rot while they tried to get their hands on his treasure, but they had never succeeded.

They couldn't take his lands, much as they would have liked to, because on his death they fell to his brother. There had been an inheritance procedure in place that prevented our family's lands from being confiscated, and it was thought his personal treasure was still safe too, hidden, perhaps buried. He had outwitted his enemies to the end, and that was what my dreams were about.

My granddad had never given his father a proper burial or restored his lost treasure to our family. Indeed he had distanced himself from anything to do with his father through fear of meeting a similar fate. But my granddad's spirit was burdened by the guilt of this omission, and those who had persecuted Guillaume were all dead. In my dreams Granddad had been begging me to put things right, telling me it was now safe to find the treasure.

When I started to question the family about Guillaume's fate I got nowhere. They had shaken their heads and said it was a bad business about poor old Guillaume to be sure, but the conversations would always veer off into other directions and never get any further.

I knew fragments of the story from the images in my dreams, and I knew a ring was involved. I had the notion that Guillaume had swallowed the ring to hide it, and that it would be found mixed up with his bones. I had come hoping to find the ring—or at least something that might help me to find the lost riches.

As the jailer swept, I looked around me with inquisitive eyes.

I had been told in my dreams to bring "all of him," "everything," and so I had come to collect all of him that was left in a physical sense in this dreadful place, but there wasn't much besides the bones. Although I knew I could come back later if I had to, I didn't want to face a second visit. I was determined to collect "everything" now. I examined the walls and the floor as best I could in the poor light, looking for stones that may have been loosened, stones that could be concealing the key to the treasure.

There wasn't much in the cell. There was an old earthenware jug—a small pitcher, standing on the floor in a shadowy corner—but nothing else, other than a few gnawed fragments of wood. They looked like bits of a stool. The jailor obligingly tossed the little pitcher and the pieces of wood into the sack as well.

"That's yer lot," he said. "Can't see nothin' else, missy, that's yer lot. Time ter go."

And with that we left the place of bones and spirits to the spiders, and retraced our footsteps until we were back in the sunlight and warmth of the day.

Broken Base of the Pitcher

The Pitcher

My horse-drawn carriage took me swiftly home. The cheerful, brisk clip-clop of the horses' hooves helped to distance me from the experience and pull me back into my life. I felt tired ... but when I looked down at the sack on the floor of the carriage I couldn't help but think about the cruelty of the lords at the castle.

I was glad to get back home to my husband.

I had married Geoffrey de Cressy years ago, when I was only sixteen, but although he was considerably older than me he was a good man and I liked my husband very much. Geoffrey was rich, and our residence reflected his position in society; he was a landowner with many servants and large estates that included forests full of game.

Geoffrey always said he'd been captivated by my beauty, but the secret to our happiness lay in the fact that we truly enjoyed each other's company. Although a little portly now, Geoffrey was still surprisingly light on his feet and had always been a good dancer, and we'd had a lot of fun together over the years. He had tried to put me off coming to the dungeon, bless him, he had told me it would be very grim—and he'd been right. But he was worried about my disturbed sleep. And so when I told him firmly that there were some things you just have to do, and that you can't be sheltered from everything in life, he'd given in and made the arrangements for my visit.

That night brought no further dreams and I awoke rested and eager to search for the ring that would lead me to the treasure. I wanted privacy for the search, and because it would be a messy job I chose an outhouse to do it in, and one where there would be good light.

I'd made sure there were no servants around as I spread out a white sheet carefully on the floor, and then shook out the sack, releasing its grisly contents.

I moved the sheet about and began turning things over, shaking the rags and bones and dust around and around until something emerged from the debris that looked like a very small ring, like a child's ring. I picked it up and examined it. I rubbed off some of the dirt and tarnish against the rough stone of the floor, and I saw the glimmer of gold.

Ah! At last!

I began to feel I was finally getting somewhere now.

I picked up the small pitcher.

It looked quite plain, but I wondered if perhaps there might be something hidden within it.

I shook it and turned it upside down, but nothing fell out and nothing rattled. I stared at it, disappointed.

Then I had an idea … and it certainly cracked open easily enough when I hit it against the stone floor.

Examining the shards, I found that inside the base there was a pattern. A series of concentric circles had been stamped into the clay, but the curious thing was that all the circular grooves, bar the central one, had breaks in them making them incomplete. And here and there, each circle was joined to its neighbors by a line.

I played about with the little ring and it fitted perfectly into the one *unbroken* groove that ran around the center of the pattern.

Was this a mere coincidence?

Or was it some sort of a map, in code, with a golden key that could lead to the treasure?

Recovering the bones had been simple enough—but the matter of the treasure was not yielding its secrets so easily ... I sighed deeply, and hoped the night would bring a dream to explain more. Not that I wanted another bad dream, but I did so very much want the treasure.

I tidied up the sheet and the bones and put them back in the sack. I polished the ring and the patterned clay on a corner of the sheet, then wrapped them in a dainty silk handkerchief and put them away in the little gathered bag I usually wore dangling from my wrist in the fashion of the time.

But then came the awkward question as to *where* I was going to keep the sack in the meantime. I didn't want my servants finding the bones—there might be screams ... or worse still, they might throw them away.

It took quite some thought before I came up with a cupboard where I was happy to stow the sack.

Avoiding as many servants as possible, I threaded my way through our house to one of its quieter rooms. Silently I tiptoed in and opened one of my fashionably ornate cupboards. I stowed the sack and locked the doors, slipping the key into the gold locket around my neck.

The bones would be safe there, at least for a while.

That night the dreams came again.

My granddad thanked me for moving the bones. He said they needed "a proper burial," because they had been "cheated of it," but he insisted they should be moved from the cupboard, and be buried in the family plot, in consecrated ground, because Guillaume wasn't guilty of anything and the charges were all nonsense.

And it was then that I saw it—the pattern from the bottom of the pitcher—it was floating above the grounds of the great house which had been home to both my granddad and my great-granddad ... and as I watched, it floated over the formal gardens toward the yew maze that grew there.

It sank down into the maze and fused with it.

I had always known that a maze formed part of the gardens, and many was the time I'd walked its paths, but I couldn't have drawn its design to save my life. I'd never given it much thought. But I awoke from the dream convinced that the treasure was to be found there, at a point corresponding to where the gold ring lay on the pattern. As I opened my eyes the words "gold to gold" were still ringing through my head.

I sat up in bed, very excited.

I felt sure the riches would soon be mine.

It was certainly true that I already had all the money I would ever need, and more, but I really wanted this treasure. I was spurred on by the challenge, curious about the mystery, and it had awoken greed in me.

I would get the treasure. It was mine by rights. *It should be mine now.*

I determined to visit the maze.

Once there, it would become obvious where it lay concealed …

The house was only a short distance away by carriage, but unfortunately I had engagements that day, and wasn't going to be free until tomorrow.

It was the following afternoon when I took my daughters with me to visit their relations in the great house. We often visited, as it made a pleasant afternoon's outing.

The south of France has an enviable climate, and Montpellier was basking in the Mediterranean summer heat when we arrived. It was another hot day in a beautiful summer, perfect for ripening the grapes on our vines, and perfect for me to express the need "for some air." So after a polite amount of time I was able to leave both my girls enjoying the social banter, and excuse myself to take a little walk in the grounds.

I headed straight for the maze.

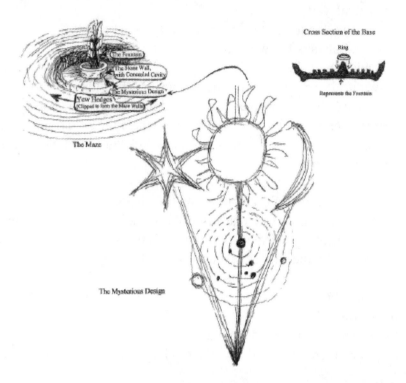

Cross Section of the Base

Ring

Represents the Fountain

The Fountain

The Stone Wall, with Concealed Cavity

The Mysterious Design

Yew Hedges Clipped to form the Maze Walls

The Maze

The Mysterious Design

There was a fountain at its center, which was so tall it could be seen from the rest of the gardens, despite the height of the yew hedges surrounding it. With the pattern from the base of the pitcher in my hand to guide me, like a map, it didn't take long to navigate the turns of the maze. When I reached the center I found that the wide path around the fountain corresponded exactly to the unbroken groove on the patterned clay.

I walked right round the circular path in the baking summer sunshine looking for anything that might be concealing treasure.

The path was paved with stone. And as I walked I found an inscription. Chiseled into one of the stones was a mysterious-looking design comprised of a star and planets. The large star had six attenuated points and was made up of many lines.

Was the treasure here, beneath this stone?

I completed my tour of the circle, but nothing else caught my eye. The stone was too heavy to lift; that was utterly out of the question. But the more I looked at the design the more its axis seemed to form an arrow, and the arrow was pointing toward the low wall around the fountain. I went over.

Although the yews were tall enough to conceal me, and there were no gardeners about, I bent down and guiltily pretended to adjust my shoes as an excuse—which gave me time to examine the wall more closely. The wall was a little mossy, but the joints between the stones were still clearly visible. I sat back on my heels and stared.

The faint outline of a square had been cut into the center of a stone. It caught my attention because this was unusual. There was no reason for it to be there. And tracing around the cut with my fingers, I found I could work the small, square-shaped bit loose— and then I pulled it out as though it were no more than a stopper. A dark cavity lay revealed.

I slipped my hand inside.

Something metal met my touch, and I pulled out a chunky gold necklace with charms hanging from it in the shape of suns and symbols.

Now I could imagine this being worn by a priest of some pagan religion. *It wasn't jewelry, it was outlandish …* and perhaps it was meant to be worn for magical rituals? I couldn't imagine what else you could do with it. It looked as if it had a purpose, and someone had obviously gone to a lot of trouble to make it …

I put my hand in again … and explored the cavity further.

My fingers found seven slender tablets of gold.

I pulled them out and found they were about four centimeters wide by eight centimeters long,[14] all the same size and all covered in writing. They looked to have been cut from the same thin sheet of precious metal.

But although these things were gold, surely the wealthy Guillaume hadn't lost his life for so little? This couldn't be the treasure. He could have given this up and replaced it a hundred times over without hardship.

There must be a lot more gold besides … elsewhere.

---

14 One and a half inches wide by three inches long.

I tried to read the script, hoping it would help me locate the rest of the riches. The tablets were tarnished and the writing quite small, but I could tell they weren't written in French, at least not the French of my day.

As I mused over my find, I knew I'd been away long enough. It was time to get back to the house.

And so I slipped the tablets into my little wrist bag for studying later. The necklace was far too big for my bag so I put it back inside the cavity for safe keeping, and replaced the stopper-stone.

Once back at the house I felt uncomfortable about my secret. I joined in the convivial conversation but was distracted. My thoughts kept returning to the tablets in my bag; I felt acutely aware of them, felt guilty about having them. I wasn't a devious sort of person by nature. I had always been spoilt and indulged by Geoffrey, and was used to getting my way over most things, but the treasure was bringing out a side of me I didn't like.

Wherever it was and whatever it was, I knew it must be a very great treasure indeed. Guillaume had lost his life for it, and the way people avoided talking about the whole affair was most odd. It was obviously a very sensitive matter, perhaps even scandalous, and I didn't know what on earth I might uncover—so I was determined to get to the bottom of the mystery *before* I started telling people about what I'd found. No, I would examine the mysterious tablets alone, at home, first. That was the best thing to do … and the thought of home made me think of my dear husband, and that brought a smile to my lips and I felt instantly better. I was looking forward to seeing my dear Geoffrey at dinner that evening.

I was glad when it was time to leave.

It was the next day before I got a chance to take a proper look at the script. But it still made no sense to me. Exasperated, I thought it was more akin to hieroglyphics than French … could it possibly be a system of writing to do with magic? Egyptian magic?

I felt annoyance rising. I had found a necklace I couldn't wear, and these bits of gold that were too important to just melt down—and it was all beginning to feel like a burden. On top of that, I had to keep them safe—and hidden.

At first I wasn't even sure I could tell Geoffrey.

But perhaps now that I had the golden tablets to show him, however strange they were, it did prove there was something more to this business than the mere phantasms of my nightmares and the workings of a woman's foolish and overheated imagination.

So I waited until evening.

When family and servants had gone their different ways after dinner and we were on our own at last, I told him the whole story.

We didn't like having secrets from each other and I felt better once I'd shared my strange discovery; but first I had made him promise to keep it a secret between us.

Geoffrey was as puzzled by the script as I was, but he wanted to help, and he offered to make discreet inquiries to uncover its meaning. He thought it possible the writing concerned ancient knowledge—as to him it had the look of Greek about it.

In the meantime, we decided to visit my relatives again.

The great houses of the aristocracy had libraries filled with old books that had been collected down the generations; and so we thought it might be fruitful to visit what had, after all, been Great-grandfather's own library to see if any of his books were still there. Perhaps they would shed light on the mystery.

I got excited as I thought about the possibilities—there might be things hidden in his books, books could be cut and hollowed out to provide a secret hiding place for treasure! Was that where it had been hidden??!

But it was several weeks before we got the opportunity to be there alone.

We had been invited over for a rather splendid lunch to celebrate a family birthday, and afterward everyone was free to choose an activity: some went hunting, but Geoffrey and I declared we'd like nothing more than to rest in the library.

When we walked into the lofty book-lined room, my eyes fell on the freshly polished surface of the reading table. Its circular top was the focal point of the room. Newly waxed, it shone in the brilliant summer sunlight, and because all books had been scrupulously tidied away when the house was being readied for the special occasion, this time the full beauty of the design of its inlaid top was revealed. Laid out before me was a depiction of the grounds, delicately executed in cut wood veneers, and there, in the painstaking detail of the marquetry, *the maze and its fountain gleamed back at me.*

I saw it with new eyes.

Did the old table hold a secret?

I had a wild idea. Had the treasure been hidden beneath it?

I was petite and agile, and as a child I'd often played hide-and-seek under this very table—but Geoffrey couldn't help but look askance as I set to, gathered my skirts about me, and began crawling beneath it.

The enormous table had many legs and the top rested securely on a substantial support structure.[15]

I crawled toward the center with great determination. I felt carefully along the ledges of the supporting framework and my fingers grew accustomed to the dry feeling of old dust as they fluttered along the struts, but it wasn't long before they encountered the brittleness of a folded parchment. It was tied in place beneath the point corresponding to the inscribed stone in the real maze.

I seized the parchment in triumph and crawled out from under the table to show it to Geoffrey. Blowing off the dust we examined it. It had a wax seal that was unbroken, which we recognized to be Guillaume's seal.

There was a knock on the door.

Geoffrey swiftly tucked the parchment out of sight inside one

---

15 It had to be big because some of the old books were huge and held maps that folded out. Sometimes several of these books would be laid out together and worked with, using rulers and compasses on the maps, when the men of the house were plotting their financial interests at sea. Montpellier is very near the coast. The maps were used to work out routes and distances so they might better judge when their trading vessels would be making port, bringing them goods and money. Also other family members might join in and pull up chairs too, and settle down to pursue their own interests in reading.

of his waistcoat pockets … and a servant brought us an invitation to partake of refreshments being served in the gardens.

We accepted graciously.

And after some cooling glasses of citron pressé we returned to the library, but this time Geoffrey insisted that we should wait to open the parchment at home, where we would not be interrupted; it would be so very embarrassing to have to explain things if we were caught with it now.

But although we spent the rest of the afternoon searching the books on the library's shelves, we found nothing else.

Once home we cracked the seal and spread out the parchment.

It was covered in flowing manuscript writing, and so, unlike the tablets, it was possible to read it:

Herein lies my last Will and Testament.

My treasure I bequeath to the finder of this Parchment, my Treasure being not of this World but of another. My Worldly Goods will pass to my Family as is the custom, but my Spiritual Goods will pass to my Spiritual Heir, whom so ever is reading this Now.

We looked at each other. Our gaze asked, without need of words, do we want to go on? I thought Guillaume was turning out to be a bit of a spooky old man, and this was more than a little weird … but curiosity got the better of us and we continued:

By now you have the Gold and therein lies the Treasure, but it is Not of the Gold, it is of that which is written and inscribed upon it. That is my Treasure, that is the Fruits of my labours of the Years, and that is what I bequeath to you, to use it how you will. But use it wisely and for the benefit of All.

And to this I set my Seal,

Guillaume

I looked at Geoffrey.

I sighed and said, "It's a bit vague, isn't it?"

I felt dreadfully let down. This wasn't treasure. Not what I'd call treasure.

I got angry and petulant as I warmed to my theme. "So that's it? So we've still got the indecipherable gold and that necklace, and that's it? Well quite frankly I could do without this. My life was going along really nicely and now there's this big question mark, this big mystery. I've lost all that sleep, I've had all those bad dreams, I've had to do furtive things in my relatives' house—and all I've got are these things I don't know what to do with ..." And I dabbed away tears.

Geoffrey put kind arms around me and did his best to comfort me.

He said I didn't have to go upsetting myself because I could leave it with him, and he would see what more he could do to uncover the meaning of the script, and that perhaps the next time we visited we would be able to find a book that could help us.

However, despite our best efforts, including looking on the high shelves, no further discoveries ever came to light in the library; and we were still no nearer to finding the nature of the treasure. Guillaume's bones were given their "proper burial" and were laid to rest in a dignified tomb in the family plot, in consecrated ground, and from then on my bad dreams ceased and I regained my peace.

The very last dream I had showed me the seven pieces of gold, and I found myself back in the maze. I was shown that the necklace had to go into the waters of the fountain—while the seven pieces of gold fitted neatly into seven little niches cut ready for them in the stones of the path at seven equidistant places, marking out the points of a star (whose center lay in the fountain).

Geoffrey and I had actually gone back to the maze soon after the dream and had had the opportunity to place the necklace in the waters and the tablets on the stones, exactly where the dream had said. Of course in real life there were no niches there to receive them; but the dream had also indicated that they were to be buried in the ground, in among the roots of the yew hedge, as near as possible to the star's points.

Before we went we made rubbings from the tablets with black wax on thin paper so we would have a lasting record of what was written on each one, and we did indeed bury them.

We'd brought a good sharp knife for the occasion, and Geoffrey had wiggled it down into the earth to a depth of about twenty-five centimeters. Then he'd rocked the knife from side to side to open up a slot in the ground wide enough to drop a tablet in on its end, standing upright. That done, the dusty soil was pushed back into place and signs of the disturbance brushed away with the tip of the knife.

This process had been repeated seven times until all the golden tablets were buried. I'd taken the necklace from the fountain, dried it off, and put it back into its hidey hole as instructed in the dream; and that had been the last of the strange things I'd had to do for my granddad.

Geoffrey had kept his word and had attempted to resolve the enigma of the script, but so far he'd always drawn a blank. He'd wondered if there was a link between the script and the university, but no one there had recognized the language either … or that's what they'd said—and it certainly wasn't Latin and it hadn't turned out to be Greek … and it didn't appear to be anything else either.

From time to time we visited Paris. I liked the shopping, and there were always things to see and splendid balls to attend in the capital.

It was very important for aristocrats like us to mix in high society and to be seen, and especially so because we lived out in the provinces, such a very long way from Paris and the court of King Louis XV. We would come for a season, and it was while we were visiting Paris that we decided to go to the king's library at the Louvre to see if we could find out something more about the script.

We took the rubbings we'd made from the tablets and showed these to an attendant at the library, seeking his help. Geoffrey discretely pressed money into his hand, and the man peered obligingly at the rubbings and went in search of a book.

When he returned he held out a book on alchemy for our inspection.

Well, I'd never been the least bit interested in alchemy myself—a time-wasting wild goose chase of a thing, I'd thought, all that fiddling about trying to turn base metals into gold. I'd had no truck with it in the past, and neither had Geoffrey. However … the attendant opened the book to pages where the seven different scripts appeared, and there were also drawings that looked like the necklace and the things on it. Apparently the script and the symbols were to do with the sun and the planets, and it concerned some sort of "Universal Alchemy."

"Well, thank goodness," we said. "After all this time at last we're getting somewhere!" And when Geoffrey rewarded the attendant further for his troubles and slipped him more money, we were told there was a society that could help us.

Geoffrey jotted down the address of the Society of Universal Alchemists, and determined to pay them a visit.

I wouldn't hear of him going without me.

The address took us to a well-to-do town house with steps

leading up to a grand front door. We knocked hard and eventually a tall manservant opened the door.

When we explained our business to him he studied our faces and questioned us closely, and only when he was satisfied did he tell us to come back—when the next of the society's regular meetings was due to be held. There would be members present, he said, and we would get our answers then—*but we must keep this to ourselves.*

The door was firmly closed and the black-and-white-checkered stones of the hall disappeared from view. Disappointing though it was, the setback didn't present a problem because we were planning to be in Paris for a few more weeks anyway.

We returned on the appointed date and were greeted by the same manservant, but this time he ushered us graciously into a gathering of smartly dressed men. That evening there were quite a lot of members present, and all eyes focused on us.

We poured out our story, all about Granddad not being at rest and Guillaume's bones, we showed the rubbings from the tablets and said that it was information we were seeking, because we wanted to put an end to the mystery of the script and the treasure.

The first thing we learned was that Guillaume had been a member of the society, and we were assured that all the members present were very, very sorry to hear what had happened to him. Then it was explained that there were different levels of alchemy. A lot of alchemists purely sought to turn base metals into gold, because that would be money and a means of living, should they achieve it—but that was not really what alchemy was about.

It was about achieving a spiritual level of being, and at the society they had incorporated a lot of ancient wisdom and knowledge from civilizations long gone into their work. To keep their work secret they had evolved their own script so that outsiders would not be able to read what their writings were about. They had devised their own alphabet, an amalgam of French, Latin, and Greek, and that was why the script had been impossible to decipher. But they said there was nothing particularly important on the gold tablets, just the attributes of the various planets.

They explained that they saw alchemy in the context of the universe, and that's why they were "Universal Alchemists." The seven golden tablets each represented a planet: Saturn, Jupiter, Mars, Sun, Venus, Mercury, and Moon. The necklace represented Sun, and as Sun is in the center of the system of planets, that's why it was in the very center of the maze.[16]

The maze itself was a parallel to do with life: life presents you with setbacks and you attempt to find your way through them, and you go this way and that way until eventually you arrive at your death—or as the alchemists saw it—your transcendence, when you go back to heaven, back to the arms of God, just as the planets will eventually go back to the sun. The maze was a metaphor for the progress of being, and it was to teach how each of us is on our own individual spiritual journey, but we are all on our way back to God, symbolized by the sun in the center of the maze.

We realized that they were saying Guillaume was a spiritual seeker.

He wasn't trying to turn base metals into gold, but he was very interested in spiritual matters and truth.

We were told direct experience of God was what interested him, and at the society they used things from very ancient times, fragments of initiations that had come down to them, to help them achieve this. They said they had a lot of rites and initiations, the purpose of which was to provoke a direct experience of the Divine, and that was what they were about, *that* was spiritual alchemy. It was alchemy where their spirits were becoming closer to God; it was to enhance their spirits and to strengthen their link with the Divine. They wanted "knowing of God," down here on this mundane level of existence, and that was the heart of it, but it didn't fit in with the views of the Church so that's why theirs had been a secret society and they had been persecuted and called heretics over the years.[17]

The society impressed upon us that its activities had to remain

---

16 Uranus would not be discovered until 1781.

17 Gnosis is Greek for "knowing of God." Earlier, the Cathars had also been cruelly persecuted for seeking this, because the Church came down hard on any threat to its power and its perceived role as the middleman between God and His children.

secret.

We were told our lips must be sealed, and that we had only been entrusted with this knowledge because we had shared with them as much as we had. But that was what Great-grandfather was about; Guillaume was regarded as a great man by the members of the society, although he was not respected by the Church of his time.

Understanding dawned within us.

Somehow the ecclesiastical hierarchy of Montpellier must have got wind of Guillaume's activities and felt threatened. They saw him as a dangerous influence who could undermine their power, and they wanted rid of him, so they used the greed of those who wielded the feudal power of the castle to solve their problem for them. Everyone knew that alchemists searched for the key to turn base metal into gold, and everyone knew Guillaume was very rich.

So Guillaume had been locked in the dungeon while they tried in vain to prise from him the imagined secret of that key. They thought he knew how to create gold. They thought that unlimited wealth would be theirs if only they could make him tell how it was done. But of course he couldn't, no matter what they did to him.

He had simply inherited great wealth.

I had listened and understood. Then I asked the society, "How does all that affect *us*? We've managed to put the bones to rest, so that's a good thing for Grandfather and Great-grandfather, but where do we go from here?" And I received the reply that we had got our answer and we didn't have to go anywhere.

I asked whether we should leave the necklace and the gold tablets where they were. The alchemists said all their members had these things. They were not old, they had been made to be used in their rituals, and they were indeed best left where they were. The site had been specially chosen for them as it was a site of significance, a site of power, to do with the energies of the land and the sun, and they had actually been waiting to be put in the earth there. Everything was complete now, and there was nothing more that needed to be done.[18]

Neither Geoffrey nor I wanted to become spiritual alchemists ourselves. Nor did we wish to upset the status quo and the powers-that-be in the Church or at the castle. I had certainly found the treasure at last, but it was not at all what I expected and nothing that I was prepared to use, and so my quest had come to its natural end.

We grew old together, Geoffrey and I, and when he died I missed him greatly. I still had my family. And I still lived in the same grand house, but with my eldest son and his family now, and all their servants.

But I was never bored.

We did a lot of entertaining, there were always people coming and going, always cousins visiting, and always things happening, always things of interest going on around me. And as I got older I looked back happily on my life and thought it a straightforward sort of life—apart, that is, from the strangeness about the dreams and the bones and the alchemists. I still had the parchment and kept it in a book in our library, but Geoffrey and I had kept what we'd found out to ourselves, because there wasn't really anything we could tell, not after the promise of secrecy we'd made to the Society.

I had made my way safely through the maze of life, and it was not long before I reached its center. One day while I was having a little rest I became aware that my granddad and great-grandfather had come for me, and I slipped gently out of life and body and into their company.

They thanked me for helping them with the bones, and for burying the golden tablets. My great-grandfather said I had done him an important service burying the tablets, because gold was

18 It was Guillaume who planted the maze and he had hoped his son would become his spiritual heir—but he was imprisoned just before everything had been completed. Guillaume had had the pitcher made, because he was going to set his son a treasure trail. In the end the best he could do was to have the pitcher brought to him in jail filled with red wine (opaque enough to hide the ring) and the kind soul who brought it also brought him a little stool to sit on, of which some rat-gnawed pieces had remained. (I suspect Guillaume had friends at the university who introduced him to alchemy, and that the books were there—either that or his son had found them in the library and destroyed them during the trial.)

the alchemists' metal that symbolized the sun, and it was a way of grounding sun energy into the Earth. He said gold comes out of the earth, but it has to be consciously refined and smelted to be useful, so it was transformed through the actions of consciousness, and then in its purified state it had been given back to the earth by way of the burial. My actions had helped to complete the symbolism of the evolution of spiritual consciousness, and in a practical way the tablets' burial helped the sun's energy penetrate Earth's body, and thus helped to bring about spiritual evolution on the earth plane of existence. That had been the point of it all … *and I came to understand that symbolically it had been a way of helping things to unfold on Earth in a positive way.*

My great-grandfather told me everyone is on this same journey of the soul, and that everyone is a spiritual alchemist, even if they don't know it! We all choose our different paths through the maze of life, but we're all on our way to the center, back to God, and that should be our conscious goal. He said that the life around us is a dream and the only thing that is real is God. My granddad agreed. He said his father was right about God, the dream, and that the only currency in Heaven is love.

* * *

Agatha's story was now complete—and I had come to the stage in the regression session where it was time to identify with "present me" once more. I watched Agatha pass safely into the light with her grandfather and her great-grandfather; and having detached from the personality of Agatha, I came to consider the message that this past life recall had brought.

My guides helped me realize that this was to focus on what is really important, and that this is definitely not "the dream." This message is particularly relevant for the period following 2012 because "the dream" will try to entrap us even more than it does already: the dream of matter—of money, of everyday life. It's real in its own way, but it is just a dream. It's like the way our dreams seem so real when we're asleep at night but in the morning they're gone. And at the end of our "life dream" we will be back with God and the "dream" will be gone and all that matters is what you've brought God from that dream. And there is only one thing God wants, and that's love. Love is spiritual gold, and spiritual alchemy is about turning things into love, making love visible.[19]

My main guide at this time, Francis, who had been my abbot when I was a monk in a previous life in eleventh-century England, helped me to understand the session—and at this point he contributed an observation about the Church. He said that there was really no conflict between the teachings of the Church and what the spiritual alchemists held dear, it was just a misunderstanding, because they were both trying to reach God, but they had their different pathways to the same goal. They had seen each other as enemies but they were not. The Church was alarmed by the fragments of old pagan religions that the alchemists used, and the Church thought everything should start with Jesus. But God is eternal and there are many ways to reach Him. Jesus came because we were finding it hard. It doesn't mean the older ways were wrong, they were just too hard for most people. Jesus came because we needed help.[20] There is no wrong path to God, but there are many paths.

For us, living at this pivotal time, the challenge is to be clear about our faith, whatever it is, and to actually be *living* that faith. For example, Jesus brought humanity a message of love, and if we had lived in the way he told us we would be in a different place right now. We wrote his words down in the Bible, but now is the time to write them in our hearts.

We need to remember them and to reawaken those things within us, because this is a time to be spiritually awake, not lost in the dream of the material world. We have to deal with it everyday, but our compass and our guiding light should be God. We need to keep our eye on our destination and ask, "Where are we going?" When we make decisions in our daily life, we need to ask, "What's really important here? Does this take me closer to God?" If the answer is "yes," it's a good decision. If the answer is "no," it's not

19 When we look at our children we are seeing love (or sometimes the lack of it) made visible.
20 My past life memories of hearing Jesus are in *Spiritual Gold*.

worth getting caught up in. And that's the compass that will steer you through the challenging times as we pass through the turmoil of the years ahead—as the energies of Pegasus engage in purging disharmony from the Earth in order to bring us a new future, one where we live in harmony with our world and each other.

So perhaps we could look at this approach as a magnifying glass, or a telescope—as something that can help us to focus, to sharpen up our view of what we can do.

Because we have already got everything we really need. We've got our tools inside us. All we need is our heart and our mind. We choose our destiny. We choose how we live our life and how we feel about the things that happen to us. So if we just add that internal clarity we're less likely to get capsized by the storms that happen in the sea of matter—when things go wrong in everyday life. And there will be challenges and there will be things that go wrong. But we need the long view. Where are we going? We're going home! We're going to God! And how do we get there? We sail on the boat that is love. That's the only thing that will take us

through the storms and take us safely back to God.

- Chapter 4 -
The Time Line without Pegasus

But time was fanning the flames of revolution, and change was sweeping through the world ...

Before the eighteenth century was out, the French Revolution would sweep Agatha's world away. Many aristocrats like the de Cressys felt the sharp blade of Madame Guillotine on their necks. The libraries of the great houses were looted and the books sold in Paris by the bouquinistes, booksellers whose open-air stalls still trade on the banks of the Seine today.

In Britain a revolution of a different sort was taking place: the Industrial Revolution. The fires and furnaces that powered an ever-growing number of factories, steam trains, and railways demanded mountains of coal to keep them burning. And as the eighteenth century slipped into the nineteenth, more and more people left the land to toil in the coal mines, factories, and textile mills of Britain; and in the grime and poverty of smoky cities they lost their connection with the magic of nature and the natural world.

Britain became the workshop of the world, and in the burning of fossil fuels and in the creation of industrial processes that caused pollution we can find the beginnings of large-scale environmental change *caused by man*. This was when the problem that is facing us now first began. It was in the slag heaps of the Industrial Revolution that the seeds were sown for the harvest our children and our grandchildren will be reaping, and it's the harvest that concerns this part of the book. *So far we've seen where we've come from*—but it's where we are going that's the problem. So let's explore time lines into the future to see where they are taking us, *and see what we can do about it.*

Of course there had been environmental changes before.

Ice Ages had come and gone and volcanic activity and asteroids had wreaked havoc. These natural events will continue, but for the first time we have added another factor. Huge economies like India and China are following in Britain's footsteps, and we have developed ever more possibilities to pollute, from nano particles to radioactivity and toxic waste—not to mention the film of plastic effluent that geologists tell us is showing up in mud sediments around the world. In their terms, we have entered a new geological age: the Anthropocene. So after a relatively stable 11,500-year period known as the Holocene, which we have been in since the last Ice Age, we are now changing things ever faster and moving into unknown environmental territory in an increasingly warming world.

* * *

As you know, in the regression sessions with Veronica I like to go on an inner journey that takes me to a door, and the door will always relate to what is coming up in the life. Consciously we have no idea what this may be, but our subconscious has already prepared things for us. I have included descriptions of the doors so you can see how this works.

The door into Agatha's session had been two doors grafted into one. A hefty medieval oak door, the sort you would find in a castle, had been given a finely polished hardwood center from the door of a great house—it was a dungeon/library split. Puzzling when I saw it, but it made sense afterward.

However, we needed to know more.

It was time for the next session.

Veronica took me back to the place of peachy-gold light and once more Hera and Francis came to be guides. At the end of the last session the objects had been covered over with a golden cloth, but they were all still there.

Tucking the two largest scrolls firmly beneath her arm, Hera escorted me out to the hallway of doors.

The first door that presented itself was compelling—all others were merely shadowy presences. This door had an old-fashioned brass knob and was covered with plates of polished ivory. It looked like a giant piano key. The ivory had the patina of age and was smooth and silky to the touch, and as I stood before it, it evoked the faded glory of Britain's lost empire, a bygone era of wanton big game shooting and lavish use of elephants' tusks for ivory trinkets.

No one had been by to polish the knob in a long while. It looked neglected and dull, instead of shiny and bright. (The reason would be all too obvious on my return.)

Hera laid the scrolls down beside the door and I noticed their rollers had ivory ends. I was given a protective outfit to wear to prevent bleed-through of the session energies. This was a dull color too, but of an antique gold, and that might sound grand but the guides were having a laugh. It made me look ridiculous. I had a shower cap, bootees, and mittens, and what I was wearing was a cross between a giant babygro, old-fashioned bathing togs, and a clown's outfit with a frill around the neck. "It's for your own good," they chorused. "You'll be glad of it later!" It was an attempt to lighten the mood …

Once before, in a harrowing session of soul-aching memories (chapter 12 in Holy Ice*), a nonphysical energy that looks like white mist had formed around me, enveloping me. Veronica is of Irish ancestry and has the gift of second sight, and sometimes sees otherworldly energies. She told me about the mist after the session, and said that its purpose was to cushion and support me throughout the recall. Well, I'd certainly needed it then.*

But this time the comforting, protective mist was back, and it had completely filled the room by the start of the session. Veronica said nothing, but she knew it meant we were going to need a lot of support, even more than before.

My eyes were closed, as I lay relaxed on the therapy couch, cosy with blankets. I had no idea about the mist or where the third regression for Divine Fire was going to take us. Just as well ... or I might not have gone.

I open the door and step through.

Extinction

The scene that meets me is so red and dry that it could almost have been Mars. And for a moment I think it is.

But no, this is Africa.

I am on a mountain.

Day is ending and a huge red sun sits low on the horizon—its last rays lighting up the vast, dusty plain in front of me and gilding my body, the landscape, and the sky with rose-gold light. A panoramic view stretches out before me as far as the eye can see.

I'm told to describe my body.

To my surprise I find I am a lion. I am in the body of a lion.

I have a tawny mane and I am male. I gaze steadily across the plain to the beautiful pinks, purples, and blues of mountains in the far distance; but no matter where I look, or how hard I look, there is no trace of what I have come to find.

This is a big landscape.

It should be teeming with herds of animals—but it isn't.

There should be forests—but there are only a few scorched trees.

There should be tribes of people in the mountains behind me—but though I'd seen where they'd lived as I passed through, the winds had long swept away their scents and voices and footprints.

I look and look. But dryness and emptiness and sadness lie

over everything I see.

And I am hungry.

I am always hungry. Wherever I am, hunger stalks me closer than my own shadow.

I know things are much hotter than they used to be and that the water has gone. Or most of it has. As I look down I can see that a little still runs at the bottom of deep gullies, trickling down from the mountains to the plain, but it wasn't always so. The desiccated water courses of the plain tell a different story, tell of wide rivers that once mingled and shone in the sun.

But not now.

There's only this now, and in a world without water the vegetation dies.

Animals relying on it for food die too. And without vegetation they can't hide, so they became easier to catch. But now the zebras and the game we used to hunt have all gone, and the parched lands lie open, empty, and dusty.

We've eaten practically the last of everything—and though it shames me to admit it—we've even eaten ourselves … starvation forced us to gang up on our oldest and weakest at first, but now our females have gone, and there are no more cubs, though they were the future.

Veronica asks about humans.

I realize the man tribes have gone.

I had been holding out hope there were still some in the mountains, or in the new land, but now I know there are no men left to eat.

They would be juicy.

But they died of diseases.

The diseases did not affect us, did not cross species.

We used to be few in number, but when the men went our numbers increased because there was no force to control us and keep us in check. But then came the time there wasn't enough of anything left to feed us, and so we've eaten ourselves into near extinction.

There's just nothing, and it used to be so different.

There are more shooting stars in the sky at night, but ever less to eat.

And we're always hungry.

This prompts Veronica to ask me if anyone's with me.

No.

I'm here on my own, the last of my pack.

There may be other packs elsewhere, but this is just an empty landscape—as far as I can see—apart from the odd bird, that is. And all I know is I've got no supper.

I don't even get the little dry, scaly, reptile things anymore. They did for a quick snack, but there's nothing. We've eaten everything and it's just so dry.

Veronica asks if there is any vegetation anywhere.

A few dead tree trunks stick up out of the plain, but although there's still a bit of green down at the bottom of the gullies, it's nothing that's much use for anything.

Things have got worse even in my time.

When I was a young cub there was more. But every year has got harder. I had crossed the mountains hoping for a better land, but this is just as dry and as empty as the one I left behind.

I'm very hungry now.

I don't know how long I can last.

Night falls.
Two days pass ...
Another day dawns ... but there is still nothing to eat.

I'm no more than skin and bones.

It's midday.

It's hot, and I am lying in the shade of a rock to conserve water and put less strain on my body. I'm too weak to go on.

There's a fly and some insects buzzing around me, but nothing else.

Sometimes the shadow of a bird flies overhead, but they're

too fast to catch when they come down to drink ... and I've no strength left to chase anything now.

If another lion came by I'd have no energy for a fight to the death ... though many a time as victor I found my supper that way ...

... all I can do is lie here ... drifting in and out of consciousness ...

... like drifting into sleep ...
... and then hearing the buzzing again ...

An hour or two pass.

And I drift out of that embodiment for the very last time.
I find myself on clouds above the Earth.
Veronica questions me.

I am in the state of expanded awareness that intensifies at this stage of the session, and so the answers come flooding in. I am still the lion, still meshed into the lion's awareness and ancestral memories but I am also myself.[21] And my present self understands that this is the future we are moving toward if we don't mend our ways—this is what will happen at some point between AD 2035 and 2056 on our time line (the exact year depends on decisions we are yet to make).

I realize we are making the world a much less hospitable place for life, because the changes we are causing have a chain effect. Beyond a certain point there is a runaway reaction, an exponential rise in temperature that can't be stopped. And in this future the delicate balance of the ecosystem has been upset and the polar ice has melted.[22]

---

21   Even in the recall it was as though I looked through his eyes with my spirit eyes, and so I perceived colors that perhaps a lion would not, especially in the red part of the spectrum.

22 Ice and water respond very differently to the sun: ice reflects the sun's radiation, while water absorbs it. Ice keeps the world cool while water warms it. So less ice meant less heat was reflected, and as the polar ice shrank, the planet heated up faster and faster. When the permafrost regions thawed, methane long trapped there was belched out, adding to the greenhouse gasses and making them more potent—because unfortunately methane is twenty times worse than carbon dioxide when it comes to global warming. And as the seas continued to absorb sunlight and grow warmer they heated the air passing over them; the warmer air picked up and carried more moisture—and so came the years of crazy weather. The overheated atmosphere dumped the extra water it carried in a series of wild storms and freak pluvial events causing flooding. The summer of 2012 brought a

The polar ice melt caused sea levels to rise. The raised waters drowned low-lying lands and changed the map of the world. Some cities flooded but others submerged, and I came to understand that volcanic activity had also contributed to the shifting and sinking of lands.

I know there's plenty of life in the seas at this time, but there is radioactive poisoning and contamination from the nuclear power stations and reactors now submerged beneath the waters. Many had been built on coastlines because it was easier and cheaper.[23] The radiation affects the sea creatures, causing mutations. (This began in 2011 at Fukushima.)

I can see there is still a little snow dusting the tops of high mountains.

But now there is less land, and that land is much drier—and this is the most dreadful thing of all, the most upsetting thing to report—it is drier because by this time the air has thinned.

The air is thinner and less nourishing than it used to be.

This means there are fewer clouds, bringing less precipitation, and as a consequence there are more deserts. But even the good soil is as dry as dust, and so it just blows away in the wind.

Lands erode.

There is still plenty of water on the planet, but now it is nearly all in the oceans and seas, instead of being generously distributed over the land as it used to be.

Veronica asks about humans.

I become aware that there are very few left on Earth at this time, and that our germ warfare programs and laboratories were the source of the diseases that wiped out humanity.

She asks if the viruses and bacteria escaped, or if they were

---

taste of this, when America was battered by super storm Sandy ... and even in Britain we grumbled about the chaos caused by repeated flooding. The flooding continued in 2013, with November bringing typhoon Haiyan to the Philippines. This was the biggest storm to hit land ever recorded, with winds of 195 miles an hour; but back then at least the atmosphere was intact.

23   Coastlines provide an isolated location and a plentiful supply of cooling water. The six reactors at TEPCO's Fukushima 1 Power Plant in Japan are an example of coastal siting. An earthquake and tsunami in 2011 triggered a massive nuclear disaster there, sending radiation round the world via winds and tides. At the time of editing this chapter in 2014, Fukushima was still spewing radiation into the Pacific, devastating the sea creatures and building up in the food chain. It has been said that the Pacific is dying.

Revising this in 2020 the situation there is still unresolved.

let loose.

I don't know—but I do know few of us have the option to incarnate on Earth anymore, and we have to go elsewhere in the universe, into different life forms and into different dimensions to press on with the evolution of our souls … although a few of us choose to return and incarnate into the sea creatures. I was the lion because it was the only way I could live at this time and see what had happened. There was no suitable option for me to be human.

Veronica asks about other worlds. Do we live on other worlds now?

We never left for a new home in the stars. There may have been the odd mission here and there, but space travel was always going to be unsustainable for the masses. Earth is the perfect home for humanity—it's our plan A, the home we're tailor-made to fit. It's our heavenly father's perfect gift to us. If we were to live anywhere else we would be in a siege situation, existing inside a small fortified bubble on someone else's world; this brings with it a withering, a kind of spiritual and soul death. There is no plan B for the human race, and there never has been.

Today, when we hear in the news that species are becoming extinct because of man's activities we may feel sad—but because it is happening to others *we* enjoy an illusion of feeling safe, but we are not immune to this process. There will come a time when there is the last human, like the last lion, because the air is changing. It's as though some huge machine has been switched on and there is less and less oxygen every day.

Veronica asks what thinned the air.

I don't know—but it is undeniable that the balance of gases is changing.[24] Over the coming years our leaders will hold conferences to talk about agreements to limit carbon dioxide emissions, and see it as a handy excuse to raise extra taxes, while little gets said about methane.[25] Deforestation and pollution will

---

24 By May 2013 daily measurements of carbon dioxide, CO_2, at a US government agency lab on Hawaii topped 400 parts per million for the first time since before modern humans existed. It has been 3–5 million years since there was so much CO_2 in the atmosphere. (At that time it was warmer than today. Scientists have analyzed ancient air pockets trapped in ice.)

25 Eating less meat would help here. Livestock create a lot of methane, and so does food rotting in landfills.

continue, and the conferences will distract from the bigger picture of our lack of stewardship for the beautiful and fragile planet we all share.

Each leader will be thinking only about their individual nation's affairs and how things will affect their own country's economy. Wanting to stay in power, they will drag their feet, and plan inadequate concessions on environmental safeguards for the years stretching up to 2050, as though they had all the time in the world. They will do far too little too late. But if the seriousness of the situation is missed, if we do not want to hear an inconvenient truth, this will be the road to our death as a species.

Homo-not-so-sapiens-after-all … extinct.

Fortunately, we are not at that point yet. We do still have a little time, and there are many people working to help turn things around. We may have fewer years than we have fingers on one hand before we reach a tipping point and begin on that slide into oblivion, but we are still at a pivotal point of choice, and we all participate in this decision, whether by our action or inaction. We can choose to recycle. We know clean renewable energy from the sun, wind, and tides is part of the solution, and we must never underestimate the power we wield when we choose to buy things. We could reshape the world we live in if we stopped buying goods and services from companies or countries that are busy murdering our Earth for their profits.

If you make a habitat different, then it welcomes different life forms. If there are dirty work surfaces in a kitchen, bacteria will grow that wouldn't be there if they were clean, and it's the same on a world. If you change the gasses in the air and change the water and the land, then different life forms are comfortable there and the ones that were, aren't any more, and so they no longer hold there. They have to go and new ones come in. It's just the Law of Life that a changed environment supports different life forms. We should not be changing our environment, it is the perfect one for *us*. Change will be for some other creatures' benefit. It wasn't their world to begin with but we will be giving it to them. Nature doesn't waste an environment, so if it will support something, that something tends to move in. This process is not evil or wrong, it just is. It will be a tragedy if it happens here, because our world should have been supporting us, but if we don't value our perfect home, when it's gone, it's gone—as they say in retail. Unfortunately, it's the only world we're going to get.

Understandably we have always had a very human-centric stance when looking out at the universe, and when considering our Maker. But from the Great Creator's point of view, humankind is just one of many, many young species. It would be sad if we go, but the universe will continue to evolve without us and barely register our departure. We may be made in His image but the stars teem with others that are too; molecules may be arranged in different patterns to form different bodies but the spirit essence that inhabits them is still the same. After all, if we can't look after ourselves, then there's really no hope for us, is there? And I am certain we will not be saved by any of these extraterrestrial aliens, whatever some people may think. Observed, yes, and subliminally educated with some DNA samples collected, but saved from ourselves, no.

The Watchers and Catchers of souls mentioned in *Holy Ice* had gone by this time because there was nothing left for them to watch or catch anymore. They got their big harvest, or at least the only harvest they were going to get, and they didn't consider it worth their while hanging about for the last few souls. They went elsewhere for richer pickings.

Veronica asks who lives on Earth in this future.

If we go the way of this time line, we will have left our world to the ancient elemental beings of fire and sea water as the changed conditions helped them prosper. They have gone forth and multiplied as we once did. But not so the elemental beings of earth and air, they have suffered. There may still be a few humans at this time, living in remote areas or in floating research stations on the seas who have escaped the plagues—and perhaps extraterrestrial creatures or their hybrids now live in our oceans and in our changed atmosphere. Those in the atmosphere could be feeding on the oxygen or simply prefer the new ratio of gasses. Covert extraterrestrial or transdimensional influences could have been behind the forces of greed, subliminally prompting and pushing people along the path to destruction. The "bacteria" may have already moved in.[26]

And what became of our guardian forces, our crystal skulls?

They were targeted by the forces of greed who didn't want anyone to stop them exploiting the oil and the fossil fuel resources, or stop them from making money from nuclear exploitation. It's all too easy to arrange car accidents and burglaries. The forces of greed thought they could use the skulls and so they were stolen to order, one by one. The skulls were not necessarily destroyed but they were rendered inert and neutralized, so they no longer actively emitted the energy fields that they should. (Picture them as the battery cells in an energy matrix that interacts with both us and the planet. Without the batteries, the matrix degrades.) But although the stolen skulls were no longer able to be of full service, fortunately there were others, including some lost beneath the seas long ago, when ships or lands sank. And even though the water muffles their effect, with their help, in total, there were still enough skulls to hold the world together, but not enough skull energy to hold it as it was.

There's no other way to put it: a concerted attempt had been made to subvert the skulls and harness their power. And when I say "thieves" you would not normally think of the rich and influential people who brought this about in those terms, but thieves they were, and worse than the original priests of Poseidon, for even they did not stoop to stealing the skulls.[27]

But the thieves did not like what they saw when they sought to profit from knowledge of the future. They thought the skulls had the power to change things. But they don't, they bring a warning. When the skulls are operating properly they have the power to *hold* things. They tried to use them to manifest things for their greed, but although manifestation is a property the skulls have, it's a subtle function. Otherwise, if you think about it, all skull guardians down the ages would have been extremely rich! Rich

---

26 In which case David Icke was right about the reptilian agenda. (If you want to find out more, look at his website or read one of his many books.)

27 Refers to events in *Holy Ice*.

in knowledge perhaps …

Their efforts were a total waste of time.

Those who did this perished when the diseases came, along with everybody else, but the problem was that the skulls were left in their laboratories when they died, in bank vaults or in lead-lined vaults, and in other ridiculous places which had the effect of damping down their energy emissions, and so they were stopped from working as they should have done. In effect, the thieves' greed robbed us all, and robbed our forever-unborn children.

The already rich and powerful had sought to use the skulls for personal gain, but all they gained was death. They were eaten by a thousand maggots and flies and learned too late that they should have left the skulls with the appointed guardians. The thieves may be nothing but dust blowing in the thinning air, but we will all pay the price for their selfishness if this happens.

I couldn't tell you how angry I was when I saw this.

The content of the session made it a very depressing experience for us, and we'd certainly needed the mist. When we played the tape recording back, my voice held qualities from the recall that sounded quite strange.

At the end of the session Veronica helped me release the fear, hunger, and despair that I was holding in my energy field, and helped me do a Soul Retrieval to reclaim fragments of my soul, spirit, and power that had been trapped in the landscape when I died as the lion;[28] but I was haunted by what I had seen and learned for weeks afterward. It was the run up to Christmas 2008, and as I did the Christmas shopping in supermarkets heaped with food, I couldn't help but think that we were on borrowed time. But there was a little ray of hope contained within the session. As I had approached the ivory door that was to take me into the African experience at the beginning of the session, hanging from

---

28 Soul Retrieval is a shamanic process. Extreme trauma may necessitate it, when part of ourselves has stuck at a point in space and time. It's like part of ourself flies out and flees the body just before death, or dissociates during a traumatic incident—it flies out and sticks because of the explosive charge of emotion surging through our being. It's always best to clear any old emotional residues that are still clinging to the fragments before re-integrating them. I write about past life healing in *Spiritual Gold*.

the doorknob was a small gold string bag containing an acorn and an amethyst crystal point. I was told the acorn symbolized small beginnings growing into big trees and referred to this book, and the amethyst symbolized protection and transmutation, which is the effect the book is designed to have on people and our future.

It was with some urgency I arranged the next session with Veronica because I was anxious to find a more positive time line in our destiny.

- Chapter 5 -
Time Line with the Pegasus Purification

When I was given the title for this book I had no idea what the content of *Divine Fire* was going to be, only that it was triggered by 2012 and the shift of the ages, but it did sound ominously like Divine retribution!

There had been a bit of a fiery theme to the chapters as the regressions progressed. The Pegasus beings are agents of the sun; the sun and man's divinity were important to the Universal Alchemists; and in the session I had just experienced, man had figuratively played with fire by playing God when he created the very germs and viruses that destroyed him. Plus the sun had scorched Earth dry through the thinning air, and the shooting stars remarked on by the lion were "fire in the sky"—either innocent space debris burning up or meteor showers ... or even ET craft visiting undersea bases.

And so I wondered what the next scroll was going to reveal, and at the first opportunity I set out on the inner journey and returned to the guides.

At the end of the last session Hera revealed that the two scrolls she'd picked up represented the two futures now most likely to manifest.[29] The one we had seen showed our future if the Pegasus

---

[29] They represented scrolls made in her temple when the Atlanteans were researching the far future using the crystal skulls. We had yet to make many of the decisions which would influence our pathway through time, so at that stage there were many more possible outcomes, and those they accessed were depicted on a vast array of scrolls, each of equal size.

But when the symbolic logic of the inner world came into play here, the scrolls' size was related purely to their potential-to-manifest score; as this grew, they appeared larger. The others in the peachy-gold place were tiny in comparison.

In hindsight all the unlikely looking jumble of objects had come into play in the *Divine Fire*

beings did not come. *Should they be delayed or called off early to go elsewhere*—thus leaving us to our own devices—we face extinction. The second scroll showed our future if they came.

Now Hera always takes things lightly. She has a very light energy and a ready laugh. As she held up the second scroll, which was slightly the larger, she threw over it a transparent diaphanous fabric scattered with twinkling, silvery stars which were exerting a transformative energy. She was laughing as she said, "The future definitely looks much better now, doesn't it?" As I looked on, the transformed energy began dripping off this scroll and collecting in a bucket that was waiting to catch it. I was wondering what on earth we were going to do with the bucket, but instead of explaining, she shooed me into the hallway to find the door to the second time line.

A big, red, shiny, high-gloss door appeared. And when Veronica asked me to describe it I noticed a golden coat hook with a little sign hanging from it saying, "open me." At first I thought this just meant open the door, but then I noticed it was actually an envelope. Inside were three golden keys on a ribbon. They were "the keys to the future." There was nothing protective to put on; in fact, I was instructed to leave all my clothes behind and to go through just as me, with no associations.

The door had three locks on it. I fitted the first key to the top one, the second to the middle one, and after I opened the third lock I pressed down on a gold lever handle and stepped through.

A forest was all around me.

Big trees towered above me, alive with wildlife. It had been raining and I was surrounded by the sounds of rain dripping off leaves. The air felt fresh, vital, and alive. Colors were sharp. I was soothed by green and I looked around admiringly, taking pleasure in the beauty that was everywhere. There were flowers here and

chapters. The basket of old tools was to help Agatha solve her eighteenth-century mystery, and the golden things represented the tablets, necklace, and spiritual wisdom at the heart of the session. The orange bag containing the violet trans-dimensional cylinder related to Pegasus. Orange is regarded as the "shock absorber" in Aura-Soma color therapy, and it helped cushion the experience of shooting through the cylinder to connect with my Pegasus self. If you remember, the session had begun with green grass in a field, a woosh of violet and then I was in space. The orange door may have linked with the bag because both the door and the bag contained the pathway to Pegasus.

there and the forest resounded with bird calls, and little birds darted about while the shadows of bigger ones passed overhead. Their bright feathers shone in reds, blues, and turquoise, there were flashes of yellow, and some glorious greens. Rain water was running down from the higher branches, to the lower branches, and then into the ground, nourishing it.

This was the Amazon rainforest, and I realized with surprise that I was observing the scene in my astral body.[30] I was accessing an experience that had taken place during my sleep-state, when I had projected here during my nighttime travels in the astral worlds.[31] Somehow I knew I had projected here in my astral body many times before. It was one of my favorite places; and I knew what was important was that I'd been here and seen things at time points in 2008, 2011, and again in 2018, but this time I'd come forward to 2030.

As I looked around me I was witnessing the changes the years had brought.

This part of the forest was recovering from a terrible fire I'd witnessed in 2011, and it was good to see that ecosystems had reestablished here.

After the fire, the wildlife had gone and there were just charred remains of trees. The smaller trees had been completely burned up, leaving the old ones sticking out of the land like so many dead fingers. But by the time of my visit in 2018 there had been signs that life was beginning again. Seeds had germinated and small trees were growing, and a little wildlife had returned to the area. But by 2030 time had moved on and the new trees were bigger and had begun to reestablish. More birds had come back, and people had begun living here again.

In fact, by 2030, overall in the Amazon, there had been a halt to the forest's destruction, and although some areas were still damaged and not repaired, there had been a replanting and a concerted attempt at regeneration. I was aware that some of the

30 The astral is one of our subtle, or you could say, spirit bodies. "Astra" is Latin for "star," and this is our body for visiting the stars, or anywhere else, as we sleep; or for traveling during meditation.

31 We can all do this type of traveling, but we often don't remember it. Precognitive dreams arise from visiting the future.

rainforest tribes had bigger numbers than they had had for years, and that they had moved back into areas where they'd once been driven out. Even the ashes from the fires had helped fertilize the soil in the end, so though it was a disaster all was not lost, and in the long run the goodness was restored to the land, encouraging future growth.[32]

This time line, the one depicted on the second scroll, the one where Pegasus was giving us a good kicking, was offering a much more positive outcome for humanity and the planet. There was a nourishing atmosphere and rain, and a sense of things repairing,

Veronica asked me to see what was happening in other parts of the world after the years of the Pegasus purge.

Traveling in my astral body I went forward to 2048 and found myself high above the clouds, looking down over North America. It was spread out beneath me and I could see that some cities had gone. Sea levels were higher because of melted polar ice, leaving some of the coastal cities half under water. The east coast had been battered by various things over the years, and quite a lot of its cities were at least partly submerged. There had been many hurricanes and there had been tidal waves due to volcanic activity in the Atlantic.

But I was relieved to find that the affairs of Man were still extant. There were still governments, laws, and a stable society, but there were far fewer people—*just the survivors.* They had learned a lot of lessons and did things differently. They caused less pollution and put less of a strain on the environment. Nature was healing herself, and there was a regeneration going on because there were fewer people. And because they had a government to organize things, technology had improved and gone greener. Cars were powered by an energy that made less impact on the environment and there were a lot fewer of them.

---

32 Trees are important to us because they give off the oxygen we need to breathe and they also absorb carbon dioxide. We need oxygen in order to live, and levels of it are falling all over the world, in both the oceans and the atmosphere. This huge area of rainforest has been called "the lungs of the world" because of the amount of oxygen produced here. But every day, all over the world, we are cutting down trees to clear the land for farming or more building. Forest fires rage all over the world, and our present way of living generates ever more carbon dioxide.

We need our trees more than ever. Fewer trees = less rain = more deserts. It's a fact.

It wasn't just the case in America.

There were fewer people in every country and in every place, but there was more of a feeling of being part of a global family. People realized they needed help from one another, so they made much more of an effort to get on. There were no wars. Well, there weren't enough people to fight them.

There had been a profound change: there was a feeling of cooperation and helping, and joint projects were undertaken where people from different nations got together to do things. Everything was simpler, and there had been a refocusing on values. People actually saw the wonder in other people. They were not just wage slaves and commodities, they were much more aware of "the wonder of the being," and people were treated as beings of infinite value.

We were more precious because there were a lot fewer of us. No one wanted to be the last one on the planet, having a lonely life and a lonely death. The humanitarian disasters that happened had mobilized aid, and they brought a change in our consciousness.

It all had to change.

The systems that didn't work—like the banks that collapsed in 2008 and the attempts to prop up the Euro in later years—all belonged to a different and archaic age. Then the governments had mortgaged the future for the financial rescue packages, and now there were too few left to pay the enormous amounts of taxes needed. These systems went the way of the dinosaurs.

Food and water were what was important.

And the Pegasus years had brought a *lot* of disasters, all sorts of things, plagues and viruses, diseases of civilization, plane crashes and other travel-related horrors, factories blowing up, and even nuclear disasters. Some were due to terrorist activity, but it was mayhem and chaos all around, with innocent people killed. During the years up to 2048 the human race was greatly reduced, through natural disasters and through man-made ones, both deliberate and accidental, with the result that those who were left valued life, and other people, in a way that they hadn't before.

The Pegasus beings achieved their aim: our values were

redefined and those who were left were living in harmony with each other, and living in harmony with the world. The Earth's call for help had been answered. God had sent the agents of the sun to facilitate a shift in our consciousness. Refined by divine fire, we were expressing more of our divine nature in our daily life.

Unfortunately, a lot of people did die.

But there's always a price to be paid.

You take a journey, you buy a ticket, you pay the price. Humankind is on a journey of evolution, and we have to pay the price. Pegasus offers a force for change, and that change is where we want to go. We can't really grumble about the ticket we have to buy, because it's our journey, and we've made the journey long and hard by our choices as a species. But the good thing with this future is that the world is still here, and regaining its health, and that the other species are still here—or at least the ones we hadn't already extinguished—and life is returning. Types of birds that were on the brink of extinction are coming back with healthy flocks, and the systems of nature are regenerating themselves in the time-worn way that they always have.

In the previous ages of the Earth the life forms have changed, but this time it's the same life forms that will be living in the coming age, but they're enjoying a spring, a renaissance of life. It might be going to be a hard journey, but the message is: there's hope.

And at the end of the day staying in body isn't the be-all and end-all of things because we always come back. We'll reincarnate here again and we can be part of the solution. We may choose to go elsewhere, but we definitely don't come to an end as individual beings. It's just a chapter in the book of our soul, a life (as I hope my books have shown). If things go wrong and it's a short chapter, well, hey, you know the next one is going to be a long one.

We have guides and angels to look after us, and they have our best interests at heart. So we may have undertaken a life of sacrifice where we do die in some explosion, for example, but it's like when Jesus came. He knew what was going to happen; and we are also divine beings, particles of God, or cells of the

Divine's body if you will, each and every one of us. And out of the largesse of our spirit we do put ourselves down for difficult missions because it will help to move things forward. Then as we evolve and life follows life, we can reap the benefits of our sacrifice. And you know there is a beauty with it, and a majesty with the way things progress. Sometimes we have to give a gift to the universe, and that's laying down our life. It's never in vain and it's never trivial, but it never goes unnoticed or unrewarded.

We need to do what we can to help others through these very challenging times. The message here is to try to make it better for the people who are left when disasters strike. It's easy to get disaster fatigue, isn't it? When it's one thing after another on the news, but the message is to never stop caring. Getting in touch with the more feminine nurturing energies within all our hearts is what will help. Men and women alike have both the male and female energies within them. For example, caring fathers are in touch with their feminine side, and it is these energies of love that will save us. When women are in touch with their male energies it gives them the drive to intervene on the world stage and call institutions, governments, and corporations to account. We can forge a new direction in the way things are done, we can evolve a new view of what is acceptable and desirable, and we can bring an end to the exploitation of both people and the planet.

Our only protection is love, so if we put love into operation and help in some way when there is a disaster, then that does protect us. Physically it protects us, it means bad karma is less likely to happen to us because only love has the power to transcend karma, and spiritually it protects us because when we're in the spirit worlds, that love stays with us—it's our treasure in heaven. We might have sent the love out but it always comes back to us multiplied. That's the nature of love. That's what Jesus came to tell us.

It is not going to be an easy ride. We've bought the ticket and it's a very expensive one for the journey we're on. But at the end of it, the world will still be here, and we'll still be here, but we will be transformed. We will have moved up to the next evolutionary level, and that is the greatest success you can have as a species.

This is the most likely positive future so far, based on the probabilities of what we have managed to manifest. But if everybody woke up from some scary, dreadful dream of the future tonight, and they said, "Oh my God, we've really got to change here," and they actually did, then we could achieve miracles, something much different to the journey that Pegasus will take us on.

But the time had come for Veronica to move the session to its closing stages; and when I came back through the door the guides took away the locks and the golden keys, because they wanted the door to be left open so lots of people could access *this* future in their dreams. And perhaps our dream life can help save us, help show us the urgency for change. But at least we do have a future to go to, and we may yet create an even better one. I sincerely hope that the plagues and even the natural disasters are avoided. Nothing is inevitable yet.[33]

I had never left an inner door open before. And although it was Hera and Francis who suggested it, I felt I needed to double check this with the Archangels I work with in therapy, to make sure that it really was the right thing to do before the session ended and I left this level of consciousness to return to ordinary reality. Michael, Gabriel, Uriel, and Raphael were united in the opinion that it was.

I realized that this is a warning to us.

It shows the path we need to take, and shows the importance of our thoughts, feelings, and actions. We all count. We all matter. We are beings of infinite value, each and every one of us, as are all creatures. Life is treasure. Life is where God wakes up in matter. A universe devoid of life is nothing. The universe exists to give homes to beings, to provide evolutionary platforms for them. Life

---

33   One pivotal day for the world was the inauguration of Barrack Obama on January 20, 2009, when he became President of the United States. The emotionally charged moment was shared by people all over the world via the TV screens in our homes. Whatever you think of him, what was important was that **relief and hope flooded into the world**. The power of that moment was intensified because collectively we sensed a shifting in our time line. It was a pivotal day, and there will have been others since then that we may or may not have been party to.

is the consciousness and the heart of everything, and as a species we need greater reverence for it. In every life form we are looking at the Creator, seeing an aspect, a tiny bit, of God's essence.

This isn't a new concept. For centuries in India the Hindus, Buddhists, and Jains have greeted each other with a gesture of reverence and said, "Namaste," meaning, "I greet the God within you who is also within me."

We already have all the knowledge we need.

We've listened to our avatars and holy people down the ages. Now it's time to integrate what they've told us.

The energies around us are changing. In the past we have been subject to brutalizing energies, and they have allowed brutal people to survive and to use that brutality to desensitize people. In the previous ages, Pisces, and the ones that went before, brutality has been in the ascendant. But now we are stepping into the Age of Aquarius, and it brings change.

Children can be cruel, can't they? But they become more sensitive and aware as they get older, they do modify their behavior. Children can be magical and innocent too. They can be many things. But they grow up and become teenagers, and go on to have loving relationships and children of their own. And so it is with our species. Now it's time for humanity to leave its childhood behind, to come of age and start living differently.

As the session ended Hera said, *"All of humanity are my children, and like any mother I want the best for them. I weep when they fall down and graze their knees, when they get things wrong, and it's very hard now watching the things that they do to each other and to the world. But there is hope."*

And she went on to say that we just need courage, and that she will be there to help us. We can call upon her in our meditations and ask for her loving guidance. She reminds us that laughter is very important, and we mustn't let things get us down—to try to laugh when things go wrong, and laugh when things go right. To take things lightly, and to be filled with light, and that will help with the challenges we are facing. "Now get on with you!" she said to me, and stood back to let Francis speak.

He said, "In times past, when things have been bad in the world, people have taken shelter in monasteries and convents. Looking back down the centuries, they've offered a refuge, and the only refuge from the world *is* through spiritual things."

But he went on to say that it's not appropriate for us all to be going and hiding ourselves away in such places now. There's too many of us for that. So it's about trying to recreate the sense of peace you find in the cloisters of that other world, trying to recreate the sense of peace within you, and to live like that in the world today. Make your home harmonious and peaceful, even in simple ways, by lighting a candle or listening to soothing music. If you haven't got a room to meditate in, no matter, create an uplifting, harmonious, and soothing environment in your home generally, so at least when you're there, when you're resting, recharging, sleeping, and eating, when you're entertaining yourself, you can be nourished in a deep inner way. His last words were, "Make your home your sanctuary."

Then they took me above the Earth.

We had with us the bucket of liquid, the transformative energy that had run off the scroll of this future, and we gently tipped the bucket so the liquid flowed out, and as the Earth spun on her axis the liquid came spinning down, flowing all over the world. It symbolized energy that would help the new future grow, take root, and come to fruition. Hopefully it might make it easier for an even better future to grow, but it's all in our hands. Just imagine what a difference it might make if people all over the world were joining in visualizations for our future, perhaps just by lighting a candle or by saying a prayer. It doesn't have to be difficult! It could really change things on the etheric levels, the higher levels of cause where things manifest first before they can become physical reality. Events happen in the world when there's enough energy gathered for them in the level of cause, and then we experience that energy in our world as an effect. In other words: as above, so below.

I'm sure there are lots of people already working for our future in many ways, those in meditation groups all over the world, spiritual healers, and shamanic healers in indigenous cultures to name but a few. Just imagine how it could improve our situation if all of humankind were to work together, if we all held a positive intention for our future at the same time.

We all tap into the collective consciousness and affect it. We all have an equal input and we can create change. We can be the yeast that makes the loaf of consciousness rise, we can lift humankind up to the next evolutionary level. We really can, or we would not have incarnated here at this special time. We came as volunteers to the crisis party on Earth, and we just need to remember it *is* a party, a time to celebrate our coming of age, and to say "thank you" to Earth for hosting it!

- Chapter 6 -
AD 2098

I got curious as to exactly *what* a Golden Age might be like, if you were actually living in it.

This meant another trip to the future.

I was still visiting the rainforest in my dream time. And I knew we were successfully changing time lines, because I'd been dreading 2011's poor harvest making food scarce and expensive. Smoke from a mega catastrophe in the Amazon combined with volcanic ash from elsewhere should have darkened our skies and reduced harvests drastically, pushing up the prices of foodstuffs and causing widespread unrest and famine in the world. It wasn't a brilliant harvest that year but nothing so drastic had happened. But I should have known that just because the catastrophe hadn't happened in 2011 did not mean it wasn't going to happen at all, we had just won a reprieve. The year 2019 would bring the fires …

However, by now it was April 2012 and spring had arrived and I was feeling rather relieved and very optimistic about things.

Veronica agreed to do the session.

Once more I entered the inner world. With Hera and Francis as guides, I approached another big, paneled and rather grand-looking door. It had a high-gloss finish of a vibrant, rich blue. It carried a central knob made of faceted crystal glass, which was set into a gold collar where it joined the door. But it was the doorframe that was extraordinary. This was a work of art. It was golden, and decorated with crescent moons, stars, and planets; and then there were flowers, trees, leaves, and branches—and the decoration just kept on spreading outward like a fine filigree tracery going well beyond the frame itself, flowing out across the wall like gold-printed wallpaper. It was so very beautiful, so intricate and perfect. It looked amazing.

The guides said these were the symbols of life.

They explained that first came the influences of the planets on life on this world. Second came the vegetation, leaves, flowers, trees, which showed how life grew—showed the results of the influences. Third, as the design spread out further, it showed the beauty of life in all its complexity. Life is golden, life is very important. Without it the universe would be empty and pointless— because life embodies consciousness and provides the vehicles for consciousness to journey through the worlds.

The guides said we choose the level we journey on.

We choose what we embody as.

We choose what we are, and in that way we can experience the fullness of the beauty of life.

This was a *door of much potential* because of all the things in the doorframe—the spectrum of all the potentials and the beauty that's framing the way in. The door is the way to the Golden Age, and that's why it's blue like heavenly sky, because a Golden Age equals heaven on Earth. And it is shiny because it is modern and about the future—but the old-fashioned panels indicate that it is also a part of history and firmly rooted in the past. The facets on the beautiful, clear crystal doorknob are the choices we have to choose from as we embody.

The knob symbolizes the diamond that is life, and if we pass light through the crystal of the glass, it acts like a prism and rainbows form, and we could incarnate anywhere on the rainbows' spectrum of color energy, anywhere in the spectrum of the dimensions, from the highest to the lowest.

Then the guides explained that the golden collar around the knob symbolized spiritual energy, and it was the Creator's signature anchoring the doorknob firmly to the door.

It certainly was the most beautiful and complex door I'd ever found in the inner world, and my subconscious had really gone to town on it—but I needed to get going. The precious session time was already slipping away … I needed to go through that door and into a life.

I'm not sure what I was expecting, but it had to be something good in a Golden Age. Didn't it?

I notice there is a key hole, but no key.

Veronica asks me if there is anything protective to wear.

I consider this.

And I find I have to leave my body behind, so I step out of it and step into strange white overalls. They are all-in-ones, with a zip up the front and a hood. The guides throw sparkly golden bits over me, like golden confetti, and I'm told this is an energy transfer!

They do make me chuckle.

The door yields to my touch.

It is not locked and I step through, closing it behind me.

I'm in space, out in the stars.

I can see the moon, with Earth not far away … I come nearer to Earth and see her clouds and her continents.

It's time to plan an embodiment.

There is a little gathering of angels and guides above the Earth—Frances and Hera are still with me and we move toward the angels and other guides. Apparently, Frances has been studying the future, and this is a golden future for Earth, not just for me, as he points out. It's the future with the most likelihood of manifesting.

Curious, I peer down. I can see Earth's still got her clouds and atmosphere, and the continents do still have green areas, though there is more desert … I'm relieved to see there's still some snow at the poles. I'm just here in my spirit body now … but it's time to come back and go into another life … so they're planning.

I realize I've not been here for a while—Earth, that is. I've been elsewhere, having lives on other worlds in other time tracks, but I've been called back here because there's something for me to do. Because of beings I know—beings I've worked with before. We have an affinity together, and there's a team being assembled.

There's a big need for teamwork now on Earth.

They're looking for potential parents, and for a window of opportunity for me to come down to them.

But at this point I don't even know if I'm going to be human. They haven't told me anything. All I know is it's to do with Earth … and I'm being taken over South America.

I'm told, "There's not a great deal you need to know. You will know if you're on the right track. We'll come to you in your dreams … if you lose the track you'll feel uncomfortable inside. Follow your heart, and you can't go wrong."

I usually get more than this! They never tell you everything or there'd be no surprises, and tests wouldn't be tests if you knew all the answers ahead—but there's usually more than this!

… Oh, it's to do with the Amazon and the trees … I'm going to be born into a tribe of rainforest people.

Veronica asks the year.

2098 … and because I'm not yet in a body and am just consciousness, I can key into the universe's consciousness, so I'm party to the Akashic Records and the general information bands that make up the universe, and that's what I'm tapping into now. I am out of body at the moment and am just consciousness keying into the universe's consciousness.

Veronica asks if the world looks different.

Bigger deserts … coastlines different … extra water from ice melt … but still remarkably similar. The map of England is different. The Wash has disappeared and a lot of the southeast is under water. Holland and Belgium have changed a bit … and a lot of islands have gone from all over the world: just disappeared. There's less built-up concreted areas, some went under the sea. A lot of cities were abandoned when water became less plentiful and land dried out, when the droughts came … and there are a lot of abandoned cities, and a lot fewer people.

Housing is very cheap, virtually free; it's just there and empty because it had been built for a much larger population. So much of it is just there and empty. People died, over time, and fertility plummeted, so there were fewer babies and there were more diseases.

Veronica asks why.

Poison in the air, food, and land.

The pesticides now killing the bees have a long-term effect on people. It's already started in our time, and accumulates down the generations, but it doesn't show up for a while.

Veronica asks if we could sort this out now.

Yes. It's especially the new ones, like the neonics—the ones that are killing the bees, and causing bee populations to plummet. Bees are like the canaries in the mine—whatever is killing the bees will kill us, but because we are bigger it takes longer. The finger will be pointed at those big chemical companies that are making money from having these pumped out over the land.

Did the pollution stop?

Yes, but only when it was too late for a big swath of humanity.

But it left us with a lighter footprint on the planet, and so we're not making the same demands, and we're careful not to make the same mistakes again. We're living more responsibly, and a big change in values happened. Every baby is seen as a precious gift now.

(I'm wanting to dive into my new life, I'm getting excited and impatient, but Veronica just won't let this go … she plows on, pushing me to find more answers. I've avoided being on Earth at the time of the poison, and felt very reluctant and resistant to seeing what had happened even as I lay on the therapy couch. I just wanted to get into my new life … But no, bless her heart, Veronica was like a dog with a bone and she wasn't letting go. She was thinking of you, dear reader.)

She asks when people realized the pollution needed to stop.

There are different time lines where it stopped at different points. It's not yet decided which one will manifest because we are still using the poisons. It will depend on how soon people wake up to the danger.

But we *are* still being born in this future, so that's good.

And when you're born, life is easier because housing is affordable and plentiful. The buildings were built quite strong, so we don't need to do any building, just a bit of repair work here and there. You can choose where you live and live in great comfort. You can have lots of space, there's no need to be cramped up.

The Internet gets much better, and there's amazing global communication, so you have huge networks of helpers and friends. Information is shared, and discoveries are shared. There's a big international community online. No one feels lonely, but there aren't actually many people. There's enough people—and they're much better organized. And we still have clouds and atmosphere and seasons, so we can still grow food.

Really, it's quite a fulfilling life, and an easy life that's available. You don't have to spend all your time scrabbling around to pay your mortgage or rent just to keep a roof over your head. You could have lots of different places where you dwell because there's so much property that's empty. A lot of it was owned by people who died, people whose entire line came to an end with them, and so nobody owns it. It's just there, free.

The earlier it's realized, the more people will survive—but it's coming to me that it's deliberate. There are people in the know who *do* know. It serves their agenda to have fewer people. And this, coupled with others' foolish greed, results in a cull of humanity.[34]

Some are already aware of the poisons, alarm bells have been ringing, and there have been petitions organized calling for the banning of the neonicotinoids,[35] but the poisoners' lobby is rich

---

34 **Consider the Georgia Guidestones**. This granite monument in Elbert County, Georgia, USA, was opened to public view in March (month of Mars, god of war) 1980. It bears a message clearly conveying a set of ten guidelines for living on the planet. The message is inscribed into the granite in eight modern languages and four ancient ones, these being Babylonian, Sanskrit, Ancient Greek, and Egyptian hieroglyphics. The first guideline states: **Maintain humanity under 500,000,000 in perpetual balance with nature.**

There are 7 billion of us at present, so if only a tenth of us were left that would still be 700,000,000. Considerably more than the declared target figure …

The monument certainly cost a lot of money and has been likened to Stonehenge because it has many astronomical alignments. Mystery surrounds it. It is attributed to an "R.C. Christian," but this is a pseudonym that smacks of secret societies. Somebody wants a lot of us dead, and they may not be leaving the outcome to chance. It's a declaration of war made in plain sight built on the highest point in Elbert County, about ninety miles east of Atlanta—remember *Holy Ice*'s chapter 7, and Atlanta's germ laboratories? There's a picture of the monumental stones and more information on Wikipedia, the free online encyclopedia. It is certainly a bit of a mystery.

35 Neonicotinoids are known to be 7,000 times worse than DDT, which was banned.

and powerful and it has swayed governments in its favor, and not just in America but in the UK and in the EU too. But even the petitioners do not yet know of the cumulative effects of the poisons, and how serious the situation is.

They get into the air and water and they travel.

The bees exhibit sudden colony collapse syndrome, but the same thing happens to people. We will have empty cities, deserted cities, with people dying because of the cumulative effects of the poisons in their tissues. There will be no babies, because these chemicals will affect fertility, and collect in the fat of the body, particularly in brain tissue and in the nervous system. So there will just be the old people, and then the empty city when they've died.

At first they'll bring in workers from the third world, from countries not so badly affected, and when they come over and eat the food and breathe the air their fertility will go too (like when they bring in new hives of bees, it doesn't mean they're going to last for very long).

The people who profit, the shareholders of the companies making the poisons, will become victims too, with what's in the air, the land, and the rain. They can't actually avoid it. But no one realizes how cumulatively potent it is.

Growing infertility has already started, but it will exponentially increase until they're closing schools because there are not enough children, and the worryingly low birth rate will be on the news.

There will be a lot of old people with no one to look after them.

The old people will be plagued by debilitating nervous and brain disorders because of the poisons. You get a bit of dementia now but imagine an aging population with dementia and no nurses because there are no young people to be nurses.

It's a bad time.

A very bad time.

Those people died and then there were ghost cities, because unless a city's got good water and land near it, there's no point living there. But all that has gone by now ...

Veronica asks if we need more information about the bad time to put in the book.

It would be a horror chapter!

I chose to incarnate elsewhere when that was going on. It just needs to be mentioned to help people avoid it ... (And by now I was getting extremely impatient to get into my new life, but the questions just weren't stopping!)

Veronica asks what people should do.

Eat organic, kick up a fuss about pesticides.

... Stocks and shares will be worthless. Today, people are focused on mortgages and property, but it's all just meaningless by this time, because there's so much of it, and nobody to live in it. The values are upside down from what they were in our time.

When do we feel the effect of the bad times?

We're in the beginning of it already. It started around the millennium change, then it slowly increases into the bad time. A lot of the damage is long term so it will only show up in the last part of your life. It shows up in young people through the loss of fertility—their creative spark, the ability to create life, is extinguished. They look quite normal but then they age, and when the body begins to break down, the nervous system and brain are particularly affected. Each generation gets exponentially fewer in numbers.

There's a lot of IVF now, and you never used to hear of that,[36] but it's a sign that it's started, and by the end of the twenty-first century it gets to the point where babies are a novelty and a rarity. But then it will level out because they won't be applying the poisons anymore—but they're still in the air, in the rain, and on the land, in the fields where we grow our food. It takes a long time before they clear.

Veronica exclaims—this is the golden future?!!

We do enter a stable time where there is a global community with communications and a lot of cooperation. Babies are being born, so because we are not using those chemicals anymore it's

---

36 Sperm counts have been falling for years. Loss of fertility has been linked to hormone disrupting chemicals leaching from plastics, and to environmental pollution getting into our water. Estrogen-mimicking chemicals build up in the food chain and accumulate in sea food too.

not getting worse; and although we may never have the fertility we used to have, at least there is some fertility. We're treading lighter on the planet and the planet is recovering.

It is a golden future for my people, the ones I'm coming to. (And I can't hold back any longer: I just dive in! I don't wait to be told!)

… I'm being born in a little village, to traditional Amazonian Indian people who didn't use the pesticides much, whose fertility is less affected.

Everything here is very simple.

The sounds around me are very simple.

I've got brothers and sisters—I'm a little baby now, a baby boy, and my name is Manannan—I'm wanted and loved and cared for, and there's quite a lot of children in our tribe. We live by the river and make our own fun playing together in the warmth of sunshine.

It is a good life in our village. We have little boats we make. We fish, and we collect things like nuts and fruits, we grow a bit of food, we have a few animals. It's a very simple life but there is education. We learn reading and writing, and there's a school with computers where we learn about the Internet. We learn a lot of lessons on the computers, although there are teachers too. We're more part of the world than we used to be, it's not just the old tribal way of doing things now. We have a greater awareness of the world, but we're happy with our way of life and there's no need to make it complicated. And there's no need to travel because you can do conferences with the computers. It's a very interactive communication. You can have lessons and go to university all without going anywhere. You just log in for the lectures and tutorial sessions over the Internet.

Cameras enhance the interactive nature of it, and it's like being face to face with people on a huge screen. We're happy living in our village, but you can have a PhD from Oxford in photovoltaics, and qualifications from prestigious universities all over the world in renewable energies and river flow energy generation.

Which I have.

And with these skills I work with others in a team to bring education and power to more and more villages. We pay for our education by collecting data, about climate and weather, about plants and their bioactive constituents; we send seeds and materials around the world, and generally engage in a benign trade with the rest of the family of Man.[37]

The universities still exist, but most are only in virtual form now. The place they originated from gives them their name, but they only really exist in cyberspace as a concept. The tutors are real enough, but they could be dispersed over the continents of the world.[38]

Veronica asks, what did you need to experience in this life?

The ease of life. You can still hear the heartbeat of the planet and yet you can use technology for knowledge, wisdom, and communication. We still catch fish and feel the spirits of the plants and live with the trees. We don't have to live in concrete jungles. So we have a life where we're hearing the planet and yet we have the advantages that the Technological Revolution did bring. (The Technological Revolution came out of the Industrial Revolution.) We have the best of both worlds. We're the rich ones now. We used to be thought of as being savages and having nothing. But we're the rich ones because the texture of our life is so beautiful. We always were the rich ones but people in the wider world didn't realize it. We're much better educated now because we've got the technology to do that without going anywhere. So we can't be fooled and tricked anymore. It's a life of beauty and ease where you can fulfill your potential and live very simply, and live in

---

37 After this regression (in 2012), I'd wondered how it was going to happen, but the Internet was probably delivered to us via balloons in the stratosphere. In June 2013 Google started Project Loon, a pilot program designed to use balloons to provide free Internet access to remote or poor areas. And it is envisaged that eventually giant helium balloons will circle the globe, using solar power to beam Wi-Fi signals to the lands below.

In the *Metro* newspaper, February 19, 2015, I found this: "A million people worldwide have signed up for free courses offered by top universities, including Warwick and King's College London. The independent students come from 190 countries and have taken 2 million '**massive open online courses**'—known as **Moocs**—since 2013. Some hope to further their careers, but others are simply interested, said **Future Learn**, which offers the courses." So, it has already begun!

38 Indeed, I got the distinct impression that Oxford's fine buildings were under water, unusable because of local flooding, and that it was purely a cyberspace university by this time.

harmony with nature.

What's important is not so much the life as the texture of it: there's the water (by which I mean the Amazon); and feeling the sun on your skin; and eating fruit still warm from the sun; catching your own fish ... all very simple, but very meaningful.

I needed to experience living like the ancestors have done in an unbroken tradition.

I needed to experience feeling I was really a part of the planet, and not cut off from it, living in a concrete box like a battery hen.

What are the pointers to guide us to this, or to an even better future?

Not using the new pesticides. And not supporting the farmers who do; it's only a few pence more to buy organic, and if you don't want a decrepit old age it's definitely worth it. For you and me that's just common sense and doesn't make a huge difference, but down the generations it does, because collectively the poisons accumulate in our eggs and in our reproductive tissues.

Sustainability has to be the watchword.

You won't need nuclear power because there won't be enough people to need all that energy. Sun, wind, and tides provide enough. The energy to run the computers in our school comes from the Amazon's water flow—it's just free and endlessly renewable. It was a team project, harnessing the power of the river; but it could be any combination of sun, wind, or water. It depends where you are, but you don't need big oil-burning generators. Alternative energy sources do get better and they're always worth investing in because that's the way forward.

Veronica asks me if I need to see anymore, or if I'm ready to leave the life and go to a special place for answers.

(After all the time we'd spent on the door and the bad time, I was too tired now to see any more of my lovely life! Afterward I meditated on it and found it was a life of happiness where I'd married, had children, and died of old age in the sun ... happy, fishing.)

The special place is back in the stars, where I was earlier.

Veronica asks if the Pegasus beings do actually go by the

winter solstice of 2048.

Yes, they leave that December.

What are the effects of their actions?

A purging: a purification of disharmony, of the ways that don't work. A lot of companies just crash, because they get sued out of existence—the poison producers and genetic engineers of crops[39] ... Things get washed away with the energy waves sent out by Pegasus. Lots of people die.

How?

In many ways, as I've said before: through accidents including nuclear ones, plane and train crashes, lots of things— through diseases, not so much the old ones as new ones from the laboratories—there's an increase in natural disasters like earthquakes, volcanoes, tremors, and flooding by both rain and sea. It's a very tough time between now and 2048, and then the chaos eases when the Pegasus beings leave. Volcanic activity quietens down, and there are ever fewer people.

It is through education that our future will be healed and brought into a Golden Age. And the virtually free and unlimited education available in this life was just the beginning. Imagine where brilliant education and our creative abilities might take us over the next centuries. The Age of Aquarius will last for around two thousand years, and the full fifth world age of the Mayan calendar will last for over five thousand. How might we have evolved by then?

---

39 Six years later, in 2018, Bayer would acquire Monsanto with its mountain of massive lawsuits over glyphosate.

- Chapter 7 -
Sacred Sites and ETs

Where we are going is somewhat amazing.

When I was searching for an answer I found this:

We were there. We were there at the party when the Earth was formed. As celestial beings we sifted the raw material of the universe fresh from the Creator. We sifted and we gathered, we selected and condensed the atoms and the molecules. We made worlds. We made the solar system, you and I and the others. The last planet we made was Earth,[40] and Earth was so rich with potential, so abundant and pregnant with possibilities, offered such dimensional depth as an evolutionary platform that we celebrated! And we were there at the party when the Earth was formed and we looked upon our handiwork, and we knew that it was good.

We plunged into the heart of the Earth's spirit, spirit to spirit we luxuriated in her richness as she coalesced and became more solid. And in the fullness of time we moved into her molecules and atoms and worked our way up through the rocks and the kingdom of minerals. We danced in the air on the breath of volcanoes, and fell with the rain and ran down to the sea. We awoke in the seas as life stirred.

After plankton and fishes came time to feel life on the surface, and we jumped on the wind and fell with the rain bringing life

---

40 NASA agrees that all the planets in our solar system were formed from the same molecular cloud, and puts it at around 4.5 billion years ago. The four inner planets, Mercury, Venus, Earth, and Mars, are generally considered to be the youngest. They are rocky, while the outer planets are ice and gas giants. As I remember it, Earth *was* the last one to be made, and was the last one **we** made, and that's why we're here now.

to the land. We entered the plants and were drawn through their roots as they reached up to capture the sun. We basked in the light they wove into their tissues, and lived in the creatures who feasted thereon.

We'd changed crystalline consciousness for other levels of awareness, and we explored all the kingdoms of life. Then came the whales and the dolphins, the apes and the family of Man. There had been input from the stars all along, as star people tended what they thought was their garden. We knew it was ours, but ever grateful for the hand of the brotherhood of the Creator, we'd accepted the best of their gifts and woven the proffered DNA into our systems of life-bearing vehicles for spirit.

Man evolved into upright furless creatures with heads shaped like the crystal skulls; and this level of the task was complete.[41] We rested and adventured through the ancient world as men and womb-men.[42]

We got things wrong and our baby steps at wielding our awesome creativity through the tiny restriction of ego resulted in Earth losing continents. Lemuria and Mu the Motherland died by fire and lie buried beneath the Pacific Ocean. Our legacy? Crystal skulls, deep memories, and the Pacific ring of fire. Atlantis sought to be Master of the World, the dominating Fatherland, and was punished when manipulated energies got out of control. In pain and in mighty rage did Poseidon drag Atlantis beneath the ocean that still bears its name. We inherited more crystal skulls, civilization, a desire to manipulate energy,[43] and a monumental

41 Man was now in the image of the celestial beings who had made Earth. (Tiny echoes of them it is true, they were vast energy beings, not flesh and blood, but they did look like us, as angels do.)

42 The gods of the ancient world (like Zeus, Hera, Mars, and Poseidon) were the dimly remembered celestial beings, our celestial heritage, perceived through our needs: we wanted gods to intercede for us, to help us make sense of the universe, to help us feel safe.

43 **The atom bomb and the nuclear industry came out of the wanting**—via German scientists taken to America after World War 2. Hitler had recreated a second fatherland to subjugate the world. His helpers scoured the globe collecting ancient artifacts of power, and the Nazi fascination with Atlantis has been a block to mainstream archaeological interest ever since. It is often said Hitler took black magic initiations to increase his personal power and his hold over people, and there was certainly a great interest in the occult in his inner circle.

Genetic engineering is also a part of the wanting. I think the Atlanteans experimented with the Waters of Life (a curiously rejuvenating spring, possibly very mildly radioactive), by mixing them with sperm for artificial insemination to produce cross-species breeding. It has been said the domestic pig was one of their successes, a human/animal cross, bred for the purpose of avoiding *rift in the seabed.*

The Earth sought balance.

She found it, she lost it, we found it, we lost it.[44]

Famine came. There was much distress to the weather and the Earth's systems of climate control. We had poisoned her and she had called for help. Help came and we regained our balance and we took the inward journey to remember who we were.

How had we forgotten? How had we fallen asleep in the density of matter so completely that we thought there was no God? That we were alone in the universe? That we had the right to poison and terminate other life forms who shared our world with us? The innocent and gentle ones. The ones we tested our cosmetic irritants on in science's laboratories, the ones whose brains we operated on, and those upon whom we committed such horrors that cannot be written off without tears? How?

We forgot. We forgot who we were. But at the end of the torment and the pain we visited upon ourselves and others we gathered the fruits of our actions. We survived the famines and fought our way back through the bad times of our own devising. We won through and we lived in harmony until such time that the Earth moved through her stages.

When the sun reached evolution's pitch she expanded and became a red giant. She reached out and took Earth into her fiery bosom. The old dimensions where we had known the rocks and the plants and the life forms faded away into higher etheric levels of being; not forgotten, always a part of the records of the universe, but like an old school uniform just outgrown by Earth. For now she existed in the realm of the sun, in the realm of the angels, higher within the frequencies of the Divine. Verily was she

---

cannibalism. Pigs are tasty and are so closely related to us genetically that scientists are looking to them to produce spare body parts for us. They are spoken of as "unclean" in the Bible, and perhaps this is because God did not make them. We did. The Atlanteans were also adept at manipulating crystal energy (and used it for more than healing and scrying), although this did not come up in my stories—but crystal energy could have been used to potentize the genetic experimental material. Think Frankenstein and lightning and electricity and piezoelectric quartz crystals.

In contrast the Native Americans, also sons of Atlantis, never forgot the lessons taught by the demise of their old land. We ignore what they say about how we treat Earth at our peril.

44 "Losing it" for man and for planet was three hundred years of the Industrial Revolution's environmental pollution, fossil fuel extraction and combustion, from the eighteenth to the twentieth century and into the twenty-first.

a place for angels now.
And where were we?
We were there. Striding about on her fiery surface, transformed;
we were great winged beings, living our lives in towering cities
of etheric crystal, singing with voices like angels as we embraced
and expressed our love for each other, spirits melding in a
divine fusion. The multiplicity of thousands and thousands upon
thousands of years of lives spent overcoming difficulties, loving,
living and dying for each other, feeling joy and pain, finding our
power and triumphing, giving birth, grieving, facing famine and
loss, hardship and death enriches us all now beyond measure: it
was so worthwhile, the experiences that had woven such richness
into our souls.

We hadn't abandoned Earth, we had grown with her.

We evolve together, planet and humankind, journeying up
the dimensions[45] on our way back to Source, returning with all
missions and learning complete.

Fortunately, according to NASA we have 5 billion years
before the sun turns into a red giant and expands out as far as
Earth, so there's no need for us to worry just yet! And it sugars the
pill to realize we will be living there in paradise when it happens.
NASA says the universe is 13.8 billion years old, and Earth 4.5

---

45 2012 was a threshold we crossed as part of our moving higher up the dimensions. In the years
running up to it, in esoteric circles there was talk of people experiencing "ascension symptoms."
What they meant was that they were feeling the subtle energy shifts that were preparing us to enter
the next dimension, which is one where we will embody more of our divine light. The symptoms
of our body adjusting included fatigue and depression, feeling deeply chilled, experiencing rushes
of heat, flashes of prickly redness sweeping over the body, ringing in the ears, dizziness, etc. (If
you want to know more use the Internet and Google "ascension symptoms," or check out a book
like *The Ascension Primer* by Karen Bishop.)

Over the eons the process will continue until we no longer need physical bodies, because
eventually we will have evolved transparent bodies of higher light. And like angels, we will not
need water, oxygen, or food then, because without a physical body the life force that has always
flowed down to us through our crowns each day of all of our embodiments will be enough to
sustain us. (It's like a lifeline from Source, and is only withdrawn when we slip out of our bodies
at death and return back to Source.)

It will not matter a jot that to third-dimensional eyes the Earth will look like a cinder. We will
have left the 3D level of existence behind and be living in the dimensions of paradise. It's like
when we look at the sun now and see only fire. It's not that that's all there is, but that's all we can
see, yet. We are caged by the limit of the dimensions we are able to experience. Bacteria in a petri
dish may be aware of the dish but have no inkling of the laboratory, never mind the universe.

billion years old. As humans only began to differentiate from the apes 7 million years ago, with another 5 billion years stretching ahead of us there's plenty of time for evolution to work its magic and bring changes to our form.

It was a beautiful experience for me seeing this future for our species, where we express our life essence in the higher dimensions and live like angels; and I can tell you expressing love while in a subtle body instead of a physical body was an intensely blissful feeling that far eclipses sex as we know it, it's an ecstatic fusion of the beings' energies with all the power of nuclear fusion.[46]

But why did we embark on this epic journey through time?

It was because we are droplets of God the dreamer who is dreaming Creation, that's the reason for us being here in our lives now.[47] We were curious, with a thirst for adventure and a craving to taste the fruits of Creation. We were not content to remain with the unchanging, perfect, bliss level of God, The Beyond The Beyond, the part of All That Is which is beyond darkness and light. No, not us; and many a time we may have regretted our rashness … but we wanted to explore everything the dimensions had to offer—and what a journey it's turning out to be!

Now, I had seen what we become at the end of time, and I'd

---

46 This is why the sun is literally a huge nuclear fusion reactor when we see it from our 3D level. On higher levels, the burning love experienced by the beings who dwell there results in the ecstasy of deep fusion. From our level we see it as atoms combining—but in its essence the phenomenon is caused by beings coming together *and expressing love*. The sun is where the most highly evolved beings are in any solar system, the sun is one step down from God, if you will. It's the God-focus in that neighborhood of the universe. The suns' light carries with it a spiritual energy that brings spiritual evolution to the planets of the material world.

On the sun there are angels praising God, and highly evolved beings experiencing love so intensely that it brings them close to the Divine frequencies. The sun is a place of divine ecstasy, and when the sun reaches out to take Earth, this is where we will be—in ecstasy—until we join God and shoot off to create universes of our own.

But by the same token nuclear fission is unutterably sad, a terrible tearing asunder, with a fallout of destructive grief. It's nuclear fission we use in our bombs and in our nuclear power stations now.

47 Orgasm is the nearest our nervous systems can get to recreating the Big Bang; orgasm mimics the melting of spirit and its outpouring into matter, the surrendering and dissolving out of part of the divine Self to produce Creation. It is a very small-scale echo of this part of our divine heritage, but it creates the conditions for another droplet of God to flow out into Creation—for someone else to arrive on Earth if we conceive. Just as it says in the Bible, *we are made in the image of God.*

understood our relationship with Earth, but the most important thing *for now* from the regression that had given me that knowledge,[48] was the significance of our sacred sites. Earth's energies are naturally focused at these key points, and that's why they were regarded as special in the first place and chosen to be places of worship. The sites link together via a system of ley lines, which loosely form an energy grid on the body of Earth (like acupuncture points are linked by meridians on the human body).

When our ancestors, who could sense such telluric energies,[49] erected stones, dolmens, and temples all over the world they were purposefully hyping up the energies already inherent in the land. Such temples were for observing the stars and scrutinizing the skies for comets (or other visitors to our world), and tracking time by marking the seasons and the ages, but their most important function as far as Earth was concerned was that they gathered and emitted her energy.

When the telluric energy had accumulated and was strong enough it shot up out of the center of the sites to form two wide bands of protection around Earth. Thickest above the Tropics of Cancer and Capricorn, the bands of energy shielded her from *negative* extraterrestrial interference, repelling and deflecting it. It doesn't mean there wasn't any contact at all, but it helped to keep scavengers at bay.[50]

---

48 The regression had happened a long time ago, but I just knew it belonged here. And when I sat down to write it for *Divine Fire* it just flowed out, and took on the form of a mythic poem.

49 It is a real electrical phenomenon. A **telluric current** (from Latin tellus, "earth"), or **Earth current**, is an electric current which moves underground or through the sea. Telluric currents result from both natural causes and human activity, and the discrete currents interact in a complex pattern. The currents are geomagnetically induced by changes in the outer part of the Earth's magnetic field (which are usually caused by interactions between the solar wind and the magnetosphere, or solar radiation on the ionosphere). The currents flow in the surface layers of the Earth, and the general direction is toward the sun, thus they flow equator-ward (daytime) and pole-ward (nighttime). (This is from Wikipedia, the free online encyclopedia.)

50 The Earth is a huge magnet surrounded by lines of magnetic flux. These flow away from the North Pole and reenter at the South Pole. Compasses use this effect, and they work because the compass needle is a tiny magnet freely moving on a pivot. One end of the compass needle is always attracted to the North Pole and the other to the South, because with magnetic energy unlike poles attract and like poles repel. It's the lines of force flowing from any object with a magnetic field that attracts or repels. Since atoms (even in aliens and alien craft) are polarized with a distinct polarity, Earth's energy field does have an ability to repel—and I'm not just talking straight physics here either, because there's a metaphysical element to the protection whereby negatively orientated beings are repelled.

But as the ancient world and its ways were superseded, the ceremonies that whipped up and focused the energies ceased to happen. Over time, sites were abandoned and damaged—resulting in the energy grid fracturing. Some ley lines turned "black" because they were poisoned by the energy of destructive events that took place on them.[51] Inevitably the protection decayed … until eventually it was too weak to do its work properly. By the twentieth century we were wide open for scavengers to plunder.

And they did.[52]

Hence all the fuss about alien abductions and UFOs that has just kept on ramping up since pilots in World War 2 first saw what they called "foo fighters." Both sides thought the balls of light following their aircraft were the other's secret weapon! But no, we were being observed and monitored.

Once we'd exploded the atom bomb we'd become even more dangerous, and surveillance and monitoring checks increased. Specimen humans were taken aboard craft for examination to see how we were coping with the radiation fallout and other toxins that were now flooding into our food chain.[53] The notorious anal probes the Grays used were part of the checkups on our health and were to monitor cellular damage.

There were also information briefings on the craft.

We weren't supposed to notice the contact, and the effect of

---

51 But by the same token they are easy for us to repair with focused intention. This is common knowledge among dowsers.

52 The Grays in particular are shifty little beings helping themselves to some "seeds from the garden" before we destroy it. That's how they have excused their activities collecting human genetic material for use in creating hybrids. They have cloned their bodies for so long there is little etheric energy left in their cells, so they splice their DNA into cells they've stolen from us and piggy-back on our etheric energy. They have been unable to reproduce normally for a very long time. They are another of the species who have destroyed their home world, and I only understood them and lost my fear of them after looking at a past life on board one of their craft soon after that event. They have been searching for another home ever since. This was part of my research into missing time in childhood and an unexplained scar on my body. The single best book on the subject is John E. Mack's *Abduction: Human Encounters with Aliens*. He was professor of psychiatry at the Harvard Medical School and winner of the Pulitzer Prize. I was privileged to meet him on one of his trips to England. If you want to know more about this subject, look at books by Budd Hopkins, Dolores Cannon, and Whitley Strieber. I made a point of meeting them too.

53 Even our scientists were concerned enough to measure the strontium 90 in cows' milk throughout the 1950s and 1960s, because our bodies were confusing it with calcium and laying it down in our bones and teeth. The Grays were concerned about how we were damaging our cells and damaging the genetic material they used for cloning.

being reconnected to planetary gravity when we were returned was usually enough to wipe it from our conscious memory.[54] But dreams of Earth exploding in a nuclear conflagration often followed a briefing, because this was the sort of scenario we were shown on screens on the craft. It was meant as part of a program to subliminally educate us out of the danger we now posed, but bleed-through occurred. Fragments of our experiences entered our dreams as our brains carried out the usual sorting and clearing functions while we slept; and we sought to validate what we unconsciously sensed was happening. We were drawn to movies, magazines, and books about ETs, and this need lay behind the phenomenal success of the *X-Files* series on TV between 1993 and 2002. The face on the cover of Whitley Strieber's famous

54 Like when you switch off a computer without saving the document. However, the experience was still on our "hard drive" and could be accessed through regression; elements of it would surface in nightmares. Generally the Post Abduction Syndrome Symptoms are similar to Post Traumatic Stress Disorder, except they particularly flag up night terrors, not wanting to sleep alone, rearranging the furniture in the bedroom, not feeling safe going to sleep at night, and a fear of night driving on dark roads.

The craft act like dimensional bridges so the aliens can interact with us, and we are disconnected from planetary gravity when a tractor beam envelopes us, floats us up within it, and takes us onboard. Tracking tags are implanted in our physical and astral bodies, so we can easily be located by a scanning beam next time they want to find us. And abductions can be physical—perhaps resulting in scars and missing time, or astral, often when we are beamed up while our bodies remain asleep in bed. I have had many a nightmare about being searched for and hiding from UFOs. It's a scary feeling when they're scanning for you, but it does not necessarily mean you're going to have a bad encounter. Often it's the team that's looking after you, and we will have prebirth contracts with them, and even dear friends on the craft. (Earth lives are very short compared to those in higher dimensions or lighter gravity.)

Taking a client back to their first encounter usually finds their team. First encounters are generally astral and when the client is in utero. Knowing your team is the best antidote to the fear that goes with the contact experience. You can "phone home" by telepathically asking them to monitor and protect you whenever you sense the scanning fear. If necessary they can put down a holding beam to prevent you being taken by others. I found this very helpful and consoling.

Remember, if they're bringing you back they're good guys. Even the Grays went to a lot of trouble to bring people back and kept meticulous records on them. They were just economical with the truth unless challenged by those who had remembered their contract, and they were ruthlessly consumed by their hybrid breeding program and their need to survive. They are really quite sad little creatures, and our fierce individuality upset their ordered world because our thoughtforms collected on their craft during contact, and over the years had a destabilizing influence on their more hive mind. (It was after they destroyed their home world that they pooled their individuality.) They lost confidence and felt it was safer. They were still individuals as we'd understand it, but most of their mind was filled by a collective thought-stream beamed out to them like a radio broadcast. They tranquilized abductees with a purpose made thought-stream too, because within the dimensions of the craft knowledge was porous. Like in a regression session—think of a question and the answer comes. You can imagine the problems we could have caused them if we'd sussed out their weaknesses and rebelled, because we are bigger and very much stronger than they are, having evolved in Earth's comparatively crushing gravity.)

book *Communion* is the face of the Grays. So ubiquitous did these characters with pointed faces, big black almond-shaped eyes, and spindly bodies become that they were even used in TV adverts. By the end of the 1990s their image was everywhere, from crisp packets to key rings and clothes.

They'd become the classic alien.

The name was due to their color.

Most contact was with benign Galactic Federation species who were trying to help us salvage our future, but the Grays certainly stretched things well beyond what they had permission to do. When I recalled my contract I had actually agreed to meet them (along with other types of alien), as had a very great many humans, because our species *wanted to wake up to the fact that we are not alone in the universe*, and meeting them at subliminal levels would help bring about the desired shift in our collective consciousness, help us to become citizens of the galaxy. But I had not agreed to the collection of genetic material. They harvested semen and eggs from abductees, and I have a scar down the back of my right leg as a result of their activities, where they once took cells from deep in my calf for cloning purposes.

Unfortunately, the wound did not heal with the usual techniques on the craft. It was too wet, there was too much blood because they'd cut through a blood vessel by mistake. I sensed panic and knew something had gone terribly wrong. I really thought I was going to die up there on the white table where I'd been laid out for examination. I was only sixteen, and still at school. I was terrified.

When they'd tidied things up they beamed me back having implanted the suggestion that I'd had an accident with barbed wire while climbing through a hedge.

I came to, posed on my hands and knees in a field by a hedge, but I was only a few feet away from an opened gate. The thick hawthorn hedge was woven through with brambles and rusted barbed wire, but there was no sign of any disturbance. I looked at the hedge in disbelief and could not for the life of me remember how I got there. And anyway, why would I have tried to go through the hedge when I could have stepped through the open gate?

There was a gap in my memory.

It was always a puzzle. An anomalous event: one fine summer's evening I was walking up a country lane near my childhood home in Frodsham, England, the next thing I knew I was on my hands and knees, feeling shaken up, and all I wanted to do was go home. It was an abrupt end to an idyllic stroll.

While walking back on the cinder footpath that ran alongside the railway track, a woman came up behind me and said, "Good God, child, what have you done to your leg?" And that's when I turned to look, and saw my white cotton ankle sock was now bright crimson and there was a very straight vertical gash down the back of my calf oozing blood. That was the first I knew about it, because, oddly enough, it did not hurt.

The wound healed quickly with no sign of infection and I did not visit the doctor —I'd been given instructions not to because he would have been suspicious about its surgical precision. The Grays knew it was sterile and would not need help.

It got me out of sports day activities at school, that was the upside, but the straight white scar that resulted was five inches long, and when I wore nylon stockings, and later on tights, it always showed through. People would tell me I had a ladder in my stockings. They were trying to be helpful, but it did get very annoying over the years … *it's not a ladder, it's a scar,* and it's still with me to this day. But the *back* of my leg? Wading through a hedge it would have been the front that was lacerated, surely. Not the back.

It was while I was studying regression with Dr. Francesca Rossetti that I came across *Missing Time*, a Bud Hopkins book about alien abductions. Ye had come home with a copy and was looking through its pages when he came across the case of Virginia Horton … and he showed me a photo of a scar she'd received which was just like mine. Not only that but she had a story to match. That was the moment I knew I had to find out what had really happened on that summer's evening.

I had the means to be regressed—I could ask Francesca.

I just had to find the courage to face up to what I might find.

Thinking something is a possibility is very different from finding out it really happened. Afterward I was in shock for a week, with my stomach knotted in fear to the point of a physical pain—because in the regression I'd seen they had kept records on me onboard the craft. So I knew it was not a one-off encounter. They'd taken me before and they would again. I'd have to go on meeting them again and again at times of their choosing. I had no way to escape. There was no way out of the situation because they held all the cards.

But at the end of that first week of terror I remembered that knowledge is power. And I set out to find all I could; I read books voraciously and explored my own memories through regressions until I understood. I remembered my contract and found my team. I spoke at UFO conferences and wrote in *Alien Encounters* magazine and tried to help others. When it's happening to you or your children the problem is fear. The key is overcoming the fear, and you can only do this through understanding.

There's one particular day that stands out in my memory. It was a sleepy Saturday morning and I'd just set out walking down the steps at the front of my childhood home. I paused for a moment and looked down at the people in Church Street ... all busy with their everyday lives. And a piercing sadness tore through me. Suddenly I knew ordinary reality could not hold me.

It was just not strong enough.

I could fall through it, and envy toward the people in the street surged through me. They were safe in a way I could never be.

I didn't know where this horrible feeling came from ... but I found out later.

This was the morning after a nighttime astral abduction. I was eighteen. I'd been plucked from our reality again. Pulled out of its comforting illusion of permanence and sucked into another.

You can see why I'm not keen on the Grays.

The shifty little beasts have largely gone now, and things have quietened down. Their hybrid breeding program was not the success they were hoping for. However ... that still leaves a Reptilian race that makes no bones about not being Galactic

Federation compliant. Unlike the Grays, they don't care a fig about us or Earth.

I'm talking here about the crocodilian bipeds who have made bases under our seas. They pose more of a problem to us now than the Grays ever did. If anyone is behind the forces of greed destroying our planet for profit, it is them.[55] They would be happy to see the polar ice melt. They are up to mischief, make no mistake, but we do get a little help with them. How do I know? Although I incarnate elsewhere in the universe after my present life ends, I still get to hear about Earth.

The information is carried by light. It's in the photons emitted by Sol.

I incarnate as an energy being and my people eat light. We devour light in the same way a black hole does.[56] When we need sustenance we emerge from the total darkness of our rest cave and we go up onto the surface of our airless world to absorb galactic light.

While digesting some starlight I got indigestion and pain.

We all did. We pinpointed where the discord was coming from. It was Sol broadcasting the pain of Earth in the bad time … and the Reptilians were there, making things worse.

The light held information about their bases.

We assembled a team to sort things out.

To travel, we absorbed the light in question faster than it was being emitted.

We zoomed down the light stream.

We invaded their bodies, shrank ourselves down, and lodged in their brains. We blacked out their consciousness, used them

---

55 Our crocodiles are what Earth made from their proffered DNA long ago, but on their home world they are the dominant life form. They have much shorter snouts and are more intelligent than our crocs. They are slightly higher dimensional than we are, they span 3D to 4D. Although we're moving into 4D as we rise up through the dimensions we're not quite there yet. I encountered these beings while doing future lives, when their handiwork was all too apparent. Both times they were the enemy. If they'd taken me, as the Grays did, I seriously doubt they would have bothered to bring me back, I might have been dinner. But in my experience not all Reptilian races are bad. There's a helpful bronze-skinned type with the Federation. I caught a glimpse of one of these delivering a report concerning Earth at a conference on a craft, during one of my nighttime astral contact experiences.

56 My body resembled an abstract humanoid shape, like the sort of stick man a child would draw. It was formed out of a black energy.

like zombies to wire up a bomb. It took a little time.

We did it surreptitiously, only taking them over for short periods so as not to arouse suspicion. The bomb was an astral crystal we were making.[57]

When it was ready we blew it. You could call it a suicide mission. But that was our job. Policing the light.

It was a short incarnation.

It took care of one of the bases.

But it did make me laugh, because by feeding on light, I'd done away with cooking, shopping, family food fads, washing up, and all the time spent pondering, "What are we having for tea?" Eating light … I could instantly see what had attracted me to the life! I used to grumble about how much of mine was being gobbled up by domestic duties, but as they say—be careful what you wish for.

Since then I've watched my words because I'd prefer a holiday life with Bigfoot, or to be back with my 5D team of cricket beings—anything but that suicide mission! But perhaps it will look different when I'm in the spiritual world sorting out my next incarnation, and working in a team does seem to be a bit of a theme for the future.

Well, I think it's best to leave the ETs here, and get back to the sacred sites that are meant to be keeping them out, or at least meant to be filtering out the baddies.

In the ancient world, spiral processions had been an important part of the ceremonies held at the sites, and the purpose was to stir up energy; ritual and intent are powerful forces. You know how water swirls in a spiral down a plughole? Well, spiral energy is very much to do with planetary energy, it's a product of gravity and orbital spin. Spirals generate beneficial energy for Earth,[58]

---

57 They couldn't detect it because it was astral; it was not visible to them. We were considerably higher dimensional than they were, higher dimensions can penetrate lower, but it is almost impossible the other way around.

All that humans would notice when the crystals exploded would be earthquakes under the sea.

58 Spirals are good for us too; use them as a decorative motif in your home or your garden, and wear them as jewelry. In the northern hemisphere a clockwise spiral builds energy, and a counterclockwise spiral takes it down. This is reversed in the southern hemisphere, just as the direction water swirls down a plughole is reversed.

and the ceremonies were designed to intensify this.

The ancient places of power are like chakra points on Earth's body, they are places where Earth's energies are naturally concentrated, and energy links run through them and connect them. Road building and other human activities, such as mining, have broken these ley lines and weakened the power grids. So not only are we not amplifying the power with ritual observances, but we haven't left well enough alone and allowed the grids to function by themselves in their basic natural form.

It is a good sign today that people are being drawn back to the ancient sites in ever-increasing numbers. Being there wakes up our consciousness, changes our energy field, switches us on. It's as if, on a deep inner level, we are being called again to listen to Earth's song and to get back in tune with our planet. In Britain, particularly, there are a great many sites, from tiny ones marked by a single standing stone to huge sites like Avebury and Stonehenge.[59]

Visitor numbers for Stonehenge are easy to check because now you have to buy an entrance ticket, so I'll take that as an example. In 2012 Stonehenge was visited by over a million people, 1,043,756 to be exact. More arrive year on year, many traveling from other countries to experience the stones at first hand. But despite Stonehenge's fame, as recently as 2007 it narrowly escaped having a road tunnel burrowed beneath it, and in 2020 this plan surfaced again. It beggars belief, but it's all too true!

If you get the chance, visit Ireland and go to Newgrange. Newgrange was a mega-cathedral in the ancient world, and like Stonehenge and Avebury, it has been designated a World Heritage Site by UNESCO.

---

59 *The Modern Antiquarian* by Julian Cope, published by Thorsens, covers over three hundred major British sites.

Stonehenge, England

Newgrange Above: photo taken from the air
Below: Close up of the entrance stone, showing the light
box over the entrance.

It's not far from Dublin and is to be found in the valley of the river Boyne. The valley holds a treasure trove of sacred sites, and close by is the hill of Tara, the ancient seat of power where the high kings of Ireland were crowned. The name "Newgrange" was given only fairly recently, being derived from the farmland it's on, while the original Irish name was Bru na Boinne, meaning "mansion by the Boyne." According to the Irish Celtic myths it was the home of a god.[60]

60 Aengus Og. According to legend he was given it by his father the Daghda, the great or good god. His mother was Boann (or Bo Fionn), a river goddess of the Boyne.

Newgrange is over a thousand years older than Stonehenge and is classed as older than the pyramids. I think it was built at a time when Atlantis still ruled the world.[61] The Bru na Boinne visitors' center has a huge car park and is well organized. Our trip there was the unforgettable highlight of a family holiday.

Newgrange has been classified as an ancient temple although it is most often referred to as a passage tomb. The first glimpse you catch is quite breathtaking. A huge kidney-shaped mound of dazzling white quartz stones sparkles in the sun and is roofed over with emerald-green turf. It covers about an acre, and the base is marked out by ninety-seven enormous curb stones richly decorated with spirals and megalithic art. To go in, you pass a huge entrance stone with an awesome tri-spiral carving, and then you walk into a nineteen-meter passageway lined with massive stone slabs that leads on into the heart of the mound and takes you to the sacred chamber. The chamber has three smaller chambers opening off it, which, with the passageway, form the shape of a cross.

In its heyday it was surrounded by a circle of thirty-eight standing stones, but only twelve remain. It has been calculated that to complete its construction 200,000 tons of granite had to be brought seventy-five miles from Dundalk Bay, while the quartz was sourced from the Wicklow Mountains fifty miles away. Imagine the man-hours that went into that.

---

61 Newgrange is conservatively regarded as being built around 3200 BC. I believe the Tuatha De Danaan of the old Irish myths were actually the ancient Atlantean ruling class of Ireland. Tuath Dé, which is an older version of their name, means "tribe of the gods."

The tsunamis generated by the inundation of Atlantis would have devastated Ireland, and swept most of the Tuath Dé away. But eventually the land would have repopulated, as settlers wandered in and intermarried with the descendants of any survivors. Hazy memories were passed down as legends: the Tuath Dé were not forgotten, and were said to have retreated into the ancient places like Newgrange, places they called fairy mounds.

The people of Ireland are what we know as Celts. Tir na nOg, of their legends, the otherworldly Land of the Young, is a place of eternal youth and beauty, an earthly paradise that lay far to the west. I'm sure this was Atlantis—home to the Waters of Life, and a magical place where beautifully dressed people dripping with gorgeous jewelry enjoyed a life of culture and ease. Where scrying skulls could show you the future and the past, transcend time, and help you cheat the fates. A land of god-like people with fantastical metal-working skills, crystals, pyramid temples ... ruled over by a mysterious all-powerful emperor who extracted great wealth from the rest of the world. Indeed, while the rest of the world was living in the Stone Age, the Atlanteans lived like gods.

There must have been sixteen people in the chamber with us, but it felt very comforting and womblike in there, and not at all claustrophobic. With all that quartz around you, you do feel good.

It is an unforgettable experience to stand in the heart of the mound and witness the replication of the moment that the winter solstice sun penetrates the light box above the entrance and enters the chamber.[62] Over the next seventeen minutes a shaft of golden sunlight widens and fans out until the whole of the sacred space is dramatically illuminated. What surprised me was how much my young children loved it.[63]

As the guide was telling us about the large stone basins that are in the smaller chambers, I remembered what they were for. The ashes of the dead were laid on them, and as the shaft of sunlight fell on the ashes any souls still remaining would travel up the beam of light into the heart of the sun, to enter the pathways of light to the spirit world, thus ensuring no one's spirit was left earthbound.

In the Boyne valley there are also sites to mark the summer solstice, the equinoxes, and the mid-points between them all.

It is an amazing place.

I have had five past lives at Newgrange, but the only one I've looked at so far was as a runner for the Druids. Taking their messages to the many small kingdoms that made up Ireland in ancient times, running through the forests, in secrecy. Messages to do with politics, skulduggery, betrayal, the marriage broking of the kings' daughters, news from abroad … and in that very chamber I'd been given "the cloak of invisibility"—secret teachings to alter consciousness to efface you from the scene. Meaning I could pass undetected if outlaws, or warriors in times of war, were encountered in the forests. It was not an actual cloak at all, but rather a mental discipline to keep me unobserved.

I was a young man in that life but I had the father from hell. I loved my job because it took me away from the village and away

---

62 This is done with electricity for each tour. It occurs naturally at 9 a.m. for five days every year, from December 19 to 23. Each year there is a lottery to choose the witnesses for the chamber. The Newgrange.com website streams this live, weather permitting.

63 "Newgrange" became a favorite game for a while after we got home.

from him … I found it exciting and I got to see the kings and their courts and see more of the world.

During the years I spent at school in the 1950s and 1960s, many was the time I tried to avoid the teachers' gaze. I would deliberately try to look like my desk and disappear. Somewhere deep inside I knew that I could, but of course I didn't remember how I knew, or even how to do it properly. But hey, I think I got away with it sometimes!

In every country of the world there are ancient sacred places worth visiting. They are like the acupuncture points on Earth's energy body, and when we walk upon them we stimulate them. We help Earth, and Earth wakes us up out of the dream of matter and expands our consciousness.

When you visit, silently ask the spirit guardians of the site for permission to enter.

You may feel your own energy rising in excitement as you approach, and perhaps sense the changing levels of telluric energy as you move toward the heart of the site. I like to take a pendulum with me to ask questions and dowse for answers; I'm not saying that it's always accurate, but it's certainly interesting.[64]

The regression that yielded this material about the sites and about our journey to the end of time was done around 1996. I've put it in here because it gives the long view. It makes sense of the struggles of our lives and shows if we negotiate the tricky years ahead and maintain tenure of our planet we will be here, living like angels. The regression was inspired by the need for information.

I'd asked, "If aliens are the problem, what is the answer?"

And I'd gone down into my body in search of the answer.

I found it in my heart. Literally, that was where I was holding the story of our epic adventure. I really do have a heart link with

---

64 Wire coat hangers can be cut down and used as dowsing rods, all you need is a right-angled shape. Make two, and hold one very loosely in each hand, allowing the horizontal side (which should be at least twelve inches long) to swing freely above each fist, and watch them move in response to the energy of the stones as you walk about. (Some people say it works best for them when the part in your hand is threaded through a plastic tube, allowing it to swing more freely. Try a drinking straw or the empty body of a ballpoint pen.)

Earth. Most of us do. And our sites are worth cherishing because they are an important part of the answer. The ancients knew this, and despite everything we've been through, we are now reawakening to our heritage, which is wonderful.[65]

I've always loved ancient places.

The first time I went to Stonehenge I was sixteen. There was no need to buy a ticket then, people just wandered about. There was graffiti on the stones and nothing to stop them from being damaged. They are much more valued and appreciated now than they were then. When I was a student I couldn't wait to get to Greece to visit the Acropolis, Delphi, and especially Knossos, the Minoan palace on Crete. At Knossos I felt I'd come home, and later I found that I had! ... But that's a tale best left for another day, and another book.

---

65 Of course we're not limited to incarnating on Earth, or tied to this time stream, but Earth really is a very special place—she's like a garden center for this part of the galaxy; and having been in at the beginning it is very fitting that we should be there at the end to see things through.

- Chapter 8 -
Bahrain: Opening the Eye of Heaven

Wherever my husband, Ye, and I go on holiday, we like to visit the special places. There's usually a delicious feeling of mystery and power there, but sometimes you sense something more.

Sometimes there's a story to be told or healing to be done.

One site that came into this category was the Barbar Temple in Bahrain.

I was in Bahrain visiting friends when I chanced across the ruins of the temple. As I stood in the hot sun reading the information at the site, the longer I was there the more I wanted to get away. The site repelled me.

Now, the island Gulf state of Bahrain used to be the fabled land of Dilmun, an ancient holy land. It was described as paradise in the Epic of Gilgamesh, and may even have been the biblical Garden of Eden. It lies off the coast of Saudi Arabia and is barely sixty miles long by thirty miles wide. It is a place where sweet waters flow and, around the coast, springs bubble up with such force that you can drop a bucket into the sea and bring it up full of fresh water. It has long been famous for pearls and was part of an ancient trade route between the Indus Valley and Mesopotamia. Sometimes it's referred to as Delmon or Telmon. The native cats on the island have DNA stretching back unbroken for forty thousand years. Their paws are webbed between the claws and they have officially been classed as the Bahraini Dilmun. Two of my friends had these cats. They can be domesticated but they always remain a bit wild.

So the cats are forty thousand years old while the Barbar

Temple itself is reckoned to be at least four thousand years old, dating from the time Bahrain was an ancient island necropolis. As I was standing looking at the battered old stones, buried memories began stirring. My subconscious was trying to protect me. It has a different take on time, the subconscious, and the fact that thousands of years had passed didn't matter. (This is why phobias can be so strong when there is no logical reason for them.) Soul memories buried below the conscious threshold were stirring—and it would take a regression to reveal the full story and the reason—but intuition was telling me to flee …

WORLD MAP (not to scale) SHOWING BAHRAIN, marked by *

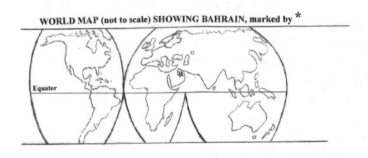

MAP OF ARABIA (not to scale) SHOWING BAHRAIN in black

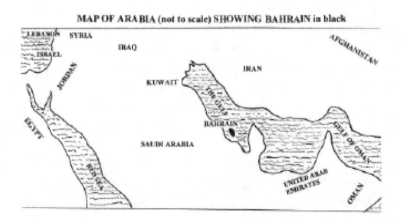

I had been here before.

Oh, yes … but then I was Akbar from a village near Thalia, and this is his story. As it spills out, a dark secret of the ages comes to light, and it is one with ramifications for all of us now.

Picture the scene: flocks of ships and boats are bobbing gently on a shallow sea the color of pale aquamarine crystal. A hot sun is baking down on dusty stones, and there I am, but I'm Akbar now. I'm at the quayside checking off boxes, baskets, deliveries of goods from the ships.

It's busy. It's noisy. There are lots of people all around me, and lots of goods—offerings for funeral services that will take place at the temple, and food to feed the visitors bringing bodies to be buried. There's a lot of to-ing and fro-ing and my job is to keep tally, to keep account. I work seven days a week, all day, every day.

I'm a tally slave.

There's never a day off … and I get very down. Sometimes I feel like drowning myself to escape.

Slipping into those clear aquamarine waters and dissolving.

But I don't.

I wasn't born here. No one is. I was brought here. Brought to the land of the dead, or should I say, "The land of everlasting life?" For here, like no other place on Earth, you may be touched by the gods.

The Eye of Heaven is open above this sacred isle, the veils between the worlds are very thin here—there are layers missing— and the gods, all of them, every single one of them, can come close and be among us. We feel touched by their presence during the ceremonies for the dead-departed-of-this-life. The dead find easy passage to the afterlife here. The gods come down to collect them and take them up to the heavenly realms—whatever religion, whatever beliefs, whatever deity it is they had believed in and worshipped in their lifetime.

Oh, yes, the gods are here.

We feel them.

We sometimes stand at the back of the ceremonies and feel a blessing when they move among us, when they walk through the temple, when they come to collect the spirit of the departed for whom the priests have called them.

They come. We can feel the divine energy.

This is a special place, very special, and so they bring their dead to us from afar, from many countries—bodies preserved with salt or dried out with hot sand, bones in jars, and even no body at all but just artifacts the person owned, or wore, that their loved ones bring when they request a service to set the spirit at rest.

And the ceremonies! So beautiful—incense and pots of sweet lilies smelling like the fragrance of heaven, gold and jewels sparkling in the sunlight on the altars in the open temple. There is no roof, it is open to the heavens.

The priests call down the gods in question. We can feel them come, they move among us and we are all touched by the gods as they search for the soul of the departed. It feels good, like being blessed. It is the only reward for such a hard, unrelenting workload.

If I make mistakes I am punished and beaten.

The tally has to be correct.

On it rests the wealth and prosperity of the temple—or so they say when they beat me.

There are only two ways to get here, money or love.

You either have the wealth to pay others to bring your body, or enough people love you to bring you themselves, as when many grandchildren pool their resources to bring Granddad. But (for just a few) there is one other way that it is possible for even the poorest to achieve this easy passage to heaven. And this is how I come to be here.

As I said, I wasn't born here. Oh, no.

I was born far away in another land, to good but simple people who believed every word their priests told them. So when I was seven they took me to a temple and gave me to the priests in exchange for their promised burial on the Sacred Isle, under the Eye of Heaven. I had older brothers and sisters, so they felt they could spare me. At fourteen I was traded on to a further temple and trained for this work. Then I was brought here with the boxes of offerings, the food, and the bodies—and here I've been ever since.

At night in my dreams I may return home, but the only escape I see is when Death comes for me. He can be a good friend, Death, and sometimes I long to see him. This life is only possible because of death, this entire society here is based on its happy outcome. So death gives me a living but I'd welcome the exchange of that living for Death himself. This gives me peace and I have nothing to fear. I do not fear my old friend Death. One day, one day … we will meet.

We work until late each day, with scarcely time to eat. The light of the setting sun is replaced by lighted torches, and then we fall swiftly into the arms of sleep out of sheer exhaustion each night. But even so, just now and again there is a moment when I catch the eye of a certain other slave and we share a joke and laugh as we pass each other in our toil.

* * *

There is the temple itself, and then there is a humble more makeshift village for us workers. Simple sleeping areas mainly. There is also accommodation for the visitors. Those accompanying the bodies for burial need food and shelter, and they may be here for days, perhaps a week as they wait their turn for their allocated ceremony time. This is a very busy place, I can't stress it enough; constant arrivals of boats and people and bodies and goods, constant departures. I am expected to work flat out, every day, all the time.

And I do get weary.

Is there not more to life than honoring death? I feel I have no life, I live to serve the deaths of others. Why did my parents listen to the priests? I pay the price for their funeral with this living death every day.

I look at the inviting aqua water and wonder, would I? Should I?

Day after day of clear blue skies and the sun gods smiling down, year on year. Many kings and important people lie here, long in the ground. There is a peace of sorts in constant work, snatched meals, exhausted sleep, and feeling touched by the gods when there is an opportunity to stand at the back and watch the ceremonies. But one day all this changes.

The busy rhythm of the year was stilled, the calls of the priests silenced.

They came in many boats. Big fierce men in swift craft. Coarse and loud and swaggering, they demanded instant service, no waiting *their* turn for *their* lord to be given his ceremony allocation. Weapons glinted in the sun as they demanded a ceremony *now*.

No one treated the priests this way.

There were murmurings of discontent but a blade at your neck usually helps a decision to be forthcoming, and so their wish was granted.

It seemed the only way.

The ceremony begins.

I stand at the back as I sometimes do. The altar is bedecked with the appropriate offerings, the singing and chanting begin but the sky grows black. Great clouds sweep in and the gentle breeze grows fretful. The wind whips our tunics about us and I shiver. The flowers on the altar are tossed about and broken. Rent apart. Great splashes of rain lash our faces and the offerings are blown off the altar and smashed to the ground. Torrential rain thunders down and lightning splits the sky.

The gods are clearly angry.

They have spat upon this lord and tossed his offerings aside.

I have never witnessed such a scene.

Rumor had it this was a cruel and merciless tyrant trying to cheat his way into the afterlife, and so it would seem. The gods did not want to receive his black soul. We stand transfixed.

The divine insult enrages the men.

They have failed in their task and been spat on by the gods.

They are angry in their humiliation, and react the only way they know how. They lash out and stab and mutilate and butcher the priests as they wreak their revenge, and then they turn their blades on us. All witnesses are cut down like a scythe through summer corn.

And me? I wonder whether to hide, to run and protect my life.

But then I sense my friend Death near and I stand and accept the blade.

Death shows me the evil sorcerers and the black magic this lord had used in his conquests. There was no place in heaven for his soul and he knew it, but it didn't stop him wanting it. His spells had caused portals to open and elementals from other worlds had come to do his bidding.

His scryers had seen this end but he hoped to cheat his way into heaven and out-race the storm. But you can't cheat the gods, they make the rules.

The Eye of Heaven shut that dreadful day to keep him out.

His followers killed the living and were not satisfied until they had burned and smashed and sacked the whole temple complex in their frenzy of revenge. Foul black smoke rose up into the sky and the Eye of Heaven would stay closed for a long time to come.

Perhaps forever.

I'd been shown enough … and the Barbar Temple was fading as I journeyed with Death through the dimensions into the realms of light.

* * *

The elementals this lord had brought through were to do with black dragon energy. The problem was two fold: the elementals weren't Earth's, so that upset the local ones, and they were destructive. How destructive I found out later.

We did two new futures for this life: one where the slave I shared the odd joke with, the only person I considered a friend, stowed away with me on a departing boat. Discovery would have meant death but we made new lives for ourselves abroad, and the second was where the storm subsequently drowned the evil lord's henchmen before they reached the temple. So the first helped on the personal level, and the second would help on the world level, but something so shocking imprints deeply on the soul of the world and is etched into the Akashic Records. After one of the talks I gave in Bahrain a lady came up to tell me a friend of hers who lived near the temple had heard sounds of fighting coming from the ruins on certain nights over the years. Perhaps a ghostly reenactment ...

* * *

It was July 2006 when I did this regression, and it was just a normal session swap with Veronica. I was looking at my past life links with Bahrain because although I'd been there before, a planned trip wasn't working out. The recall showed me why, and the guides said that the energy I carried from the past would aggravate the storm energy gathering in the region.

I realized it was not the right time to go.

The war in Iraq had stirred up a hornets' nest bringing death and destruction to that part of the world, and the turmoil was far from over. By 2006 there was almost a civil war going on in Iraq, and unrest was rippling throughout the Arab world. Bahrain was to prove no exception to this.

My friends did a group meditation there to close the portals and bring healing into the situation with the elementals. So at least that was a good thing to come out of the regression, even though I knew it was not wise for me to go. The following year I began writing my book, and the years slipped past as I was engrossed in the research, writing up the sessions, and working on draft after draft of the manuscript.

But by January 2013, with the 2012 winter solstice safely behind us, things had changed. The troubles in Bahrain had come to a head in 2011 with the occupation of Pearl Roundabout. That was now demolished and things were calming down.

I had been invited again, and call me daft, but I only realized the real reason I was going a few days before I went. I was lying in bed, drifting off to sleep, when the penny dropped. I dug out the Barbar notes the next day and wrote a short guided meditation to take with me.

There was healing to be done.

The time was right.

As soon as I arrived I noticed a difference. It was much harder to get the entry visa at the airport because the officials were more suspicious of visitors. And when I traveled through Manama, the capital city, I couldn't help but notice the traffic chaos caused by youths who'd set fire to piles of old tires in the roads. The flames of unrest had been fanned by Iran and there was talk of tear gas being used to break up mobs. I didn't see that, but in Manama roads were closed off, traffic was diverted, and there was gridlock—but what horrified me most was seeing the columns of black smoke rising up into the clear blue sky. This might be January 2013 but I'd seen that black smoke before—it had marked the destruction of the temple. And to see it again on the Sacred Isle was appalling. It wasn't just a few old tires—powerful ancient forces of destruction were being stirred up by envy and hate.

In the Country Mall in Budaiya (an area at the heart of the troubles), I gave an evening talk and a demonstration of past life therapy to an invited audience. I shared my story about the sack of the Barbar Temple and invited the people present to join with me in a guided meditation to begin a process to reopen the Eye and cleanse the black energy from the land.

And this was repeated a few days later with those who came to the Mind, Body, Spirit morning my friends organize in the Mall each month.

So the healing has started and it is an ongoing process.

Only so much change is comfortable at any one time, so it's best done little and often to allow for a smoother transition. With this in mind, I encouraged those who took part to continue the work in their own personal prayers—and I welcome anyone, anywhere, to join in when they have a quiet moment. We can heal the world and free the future. Nothing has to be, and intention is everything when it comes to healing work.

A new age is beginning.

We are crossing the threshold, and it is time for the Eye of Heaven to be open once more. We are at a pivotal point in our spiritual evolution, and divine energy and grace flowing to us through the Eye can bring peace and harmony, not just to Bahrain, but to the whole Gulf region and to the world.

I feel strongly that opening the Eye is one of the keys to ushering in the Golden Age.

Our future on this planet is hanging in the balance, and what we do now and in the next few years will matter as never before.

Atlantis perished because of rigid thinking. The Atlanteans were afraid to break with thousands of years of tradition and do things in a new way. We aren't. We are used to living in a rapidly changing world where a flexible and creative approach to problem solving brings us progress and rewards. So even if you've never meditated before, try this. It's very simple. There are echoes of destruction stalking the world that are seeking a second Atlantis. Don't let them win. This time let it be us that changes, not the world that has change forced upon it.

This is a simple version of the visualization and prayer I used in Bahrain. It only takes a few minutes, and if you would like to help change unfold, please feel free to use it. (And feel free to share it with others.) It also has its own page at the end of the book.

Make yourself comfortable. Switch off your phone.

Close your eyes. Settle down into your prayer mode … and begin.

Visualization and Prayer
to Help Heal our World

Picture God's light flowing down from the heavenly realms and surrounding you, keeping you safe.

Ask the Archangels Michael, Uriel, Gabriel, and Raphael and their legions of angels to be with you to help you in your endeavor.

Ask them to take away the old stuck energies from past traumas that may be lodged in our sacred sites (like Bahrain), and add whichever others you would like to heal as well, to help return them to their full guardian capacity—visualize angels joining in with you, as you pull out the remnants of old black energy as though they were nothing more than bits of black ribbon, and picture legions of angels taking this back to Source to be recycled and transmuted back into pure divine energy. Visualize them taking it all away, just see it go.

Now picture heavenly light flowing down into Bahrain and into the sacred sites you've chosen, down through the dimensions— the Creator's light, penetrating matter like shafts of sunlight through clouds ... Light everywhere, spilling out in a tide of love and joy that flows right around the world, healing and rebalancing everywhere. Light flowing down and into the energy grids and veins of the world, coursing through our sacred sites (especially the ones you've picked).

Then ask God to:

Deliver us now from the sins of the past and the wounds of the world.

Cleanse our spirits and our souls and our lands.

Renew us. Renew us with the Creator's light, and may we be blessed, and may this land be blessed.

May the Eye of Heaven be open once more—and may God's light flow down into the world through it.

May Divine Grace pour forth, bringing peace and

harmony and healing, so that humanity may enter a Golden Age, a time when we live in harmony with the Earth and all its creatures.

And I accept that it is done.
I thank the angels. Amen. (So be it.)

Very simple, but imagine the changes we could bring about together. We could be a worldwide team, an army of light.

* * *

Well, so far we've looked into the near future, but though I'd greeted Pegasus at the solstice and had hope in my heart that the Pegasus beings were coming—*I did not yet know if they were here.* Had they actually come? Did we have a future to go to? — Was the time line of the second scroll going to manifest, or were we condemned to the miserable end of the first?

I couldn't bear to look before my trip to Bahrain.

But after returning I had to know.

I meditated and met the guides.

Jesus,[66] Hera, and Frances took me back to that windy solstice morning on the northeast coast of England. In my astral body I soared high above Earth's northern hemisphere.

I looked down.

Far below us, flocks of Pegasus beings were spiraling gracefully around and around our world. I was mesmerized and moved by their fluid beauty.

As I gazed at them Hera said, "Isn't it wonderful!" (She meant, *that they'd come.*)

Jesus said, "It's an expression of my Father's love" (*for humanity*).

And Francis said, "It will tear down what isn't real—the seemingly 'correct'—it will reveal hypocrisy in things, especially in the Church ... and as for the Pegasus beings, it's like they sing

---

66 Jesus has been a guide intermittently for the books, only for certain sessions. But he came into this meditation.

a song—they hold a note and disharmony crumbles. But just don't be in the way when things crumble and fall! They will lift the hum of the planet."

I was so relieved.

I hadn't dared look any earlier.

Within weeks I came across an article on the BBC news that said although we can't hear it, the Earth is permanently humming—and researchers in Finland have recorded this background noise. Seismic waves created by oceans, rain, wind, and loud human activity have combined to create a humming that the scientists are hoping will shed light on the planet's deep interior and help us to understand more about the geology of the Earth's mantle. Well then, Earth hums, it's official. It will be interesting to see if the hum changes over the next few decades. The study was detailed in the November 23, 2012, issue of the journal *Science*, and the data came from forty-two recording stations in northern Finland. It got picked up by the news a couple of months later, but you can still find the information on the web. See www.livescience. com/25014-seismic-noise-earth-interior.html (10.4.2014).

But it comes to something when you're grateful that your species is going to be drastically reduced in numbers and endure disasters—and of course we still have the option to use our free will … we could make things even worse!

However, there was something else I needed to do following on from the visit to Bahrain. I was on the trail of the last key.

- Chapter 9 -
The Last Key

On my trip in January 2013 I'd visited another set of ruins in Bahrain, this time near the Bahrain Fort. And there I found Barbar was not the only temple!

My friend Julie Lomas had brought me to the fort to have coffee at a pretty café by the sea, only to find it closed because of the troubles. It was a lovely day so we went for a stroll. The café was only a stone's throw away from a recent archaeological dig. Idly curious, we walked the pathway round the excavations, and it was an exquisite feeling just to be there. I stood in the sunshine with Julie and felt waves of peace radiating from the ancient site. It was quite extraordinary. I've never experienced anything like it anywhere else in the world. I sensed a strong past life connection—but it couldn't have been more different from my experience at Barbar. This time I didn't want to leave.

Later that year, when there was talk of my returning to Bahrain in 2014, I wanted to research this further. I decided to do a regression.

The Internet told me that the ruins were a UNESCO World Heritage Site where excavations had already gone back five thousand years revealing seven civilizations of urban structures. Relics of copper and ivory unearthed served to demonstrate the extensive trading links enjoyed in the ancient world … It was a site with a rich history, but Veronica was busy. This time it was Ye who took me into the inner world to find hidden memories buried in the depths of my soul. He'd been so intrigued by my work that he was now a past life therapist himself, having studied on one of my training courses. He used the shamanic pathway I'd learned with Dr. Francesca Rossetti (written about in *Spiritual Gold*). With this style of work, after a deep relaxation you visualize yourself in a beautiful place in nature, and then go on a journey to your chosen destination. Your body becomes a shaman body, the gateway to your soul memories.

The place in nature came spontaneously and reminded me of happy childhood memories. It was like the hill where I grew up in England. I felt I was in the warmth of a sunny afternoon, and the air was heavy with the smell of wet bracken and the richness of damp, peaty leaf mould. I found myself standing on a sandy pathway surrounded by russet-red bracken and oak trees still clad in the green-gold leaves of autumn.

My guardian angel and I followed the path into a sandstone cave. There were steps carved into the stone, and I visualized myself descending them until I stood on a sandy floor.

Ye asks me to contact the spirit of the cave, the guardian of the inner world.

It comes in the form of a wolf. The wolf has thick fur and kind eyes—and I recognize him to be a power animal of mine. He says he has come to help me hunt down my true purpose. (I had lost this over the summer and had stalled finishing my book. In June I'd had an operation to replace a joint in my foot, a toe joint, but after that, although I did other things, I couldn't get back to the book. I couldn't take it forward.) I ask the wolf to open the sandy floor for me, and I visualize floating through it and down into my own body through my crown, and as I scan through my body looking for the main area linked to my past life at the temple near the fort, I find it to be my heart.

Ye asks me what emotion I am holding there, linking me to the life.

The answer comes as "happiness and fulfillment." And in that moment, although I still have no idea what the story is going to reveal, I just know it is a life where I had fulfilled my purpose.

Ye asks me to look at my feet, and to tell him what I see.

"Sandals ... women's feet," comes my reply. And when I look to see what else I am wearing, it is a simple blue robe with no sleeves, although a thin piece of white fabric drapes around my shoulders, covering my arms to the elbow. It's just a simple white rectangle, slit in the center to pass over my head.

Ye asks my name and asks what I am doing.

My name is An-hara and I am watching something.

I am inside the temple.

Partly concealed in the shadows of a covered walkway, I am watching a ceremony being conducted by the light of a full moon.

There are a lot of people here, including parents with young children, all crowded into a part of the temple complex that is open to the heavens. Petals, flowers, herbs, incense resin, and heaps of sweet smelling, starry-white jasmine blossoms are strewn on an altar as offerings to The Goddess.

Ye asks me which one, which goddess.

Shocked, I answer <u>The</u> Goddess, Mother of all Life. It is She we worship here. It is Her temple. … This is a Goddess Temple, and it is my home.

And with this knowledge comes the awareness that this is before the Barbar Temple ever came to be … this is a long time ago, when The Goddess was universally worshipped in the world. When we could see Her in the landscape, when we knew the swells and folds of Earth as Her body. Our lush and fertile lands are very sacred, for we all suckle at the breast of The Great Mother. We feed off Her bounty with every mouthful of food and every sip of water that we take …

I am witnessing a Full Moon Ceremony. It is for giving thanks.

There is chanting and singing as the gifts She has given us during the last moon are acknowledged. Word has been sent to us of babies successfully conceived after our help, and their mothers' names and lineage are called out along with those who have been born. There are many young children here now because when they are five years old their parents bring them to the ceremony, in thanksgiving for having been blessed by The Great Mother.

A lot of women come here who want babies and are having trouble conceiving. They come for a moon in the hope of conceiving on their return home. We do our best to help them, and there is a special area where we work with them using dreams and rituals, medicinal herbs and thalasso therapy—involving hot seawater and heated stones.

Others come here to give birth, but everyone comes to give thanks to The Goddess. Husbands and fathers and brothers come too. Men give offerings for their offspring. There are rituals for the fertility of men, and for the fertility of the land, the people, and the animals.

It is our job to uncover the causes of problems with fertility.

Fertility is gifted to the world by The Great Mother, and we intercede with Her on their behalf. I am one of the priestesses here, and we all wear the blue and the white … but I'm not needed at this ceremony and so I'm watching from the back, just appreciating the beauty and the joy of it all. I feel so peaceful. I feel assured and confident in my gifts. I know I can help people, and that makes me happy.

The chief priestess, Mother of the Temple, is taking the ceremony. She is the one closest to The Goddess. (In the sense that being the oldest, she is the one who will be seeing Her the soonest.)

Ye asks how long I've been here.

I've been here all my life and now I'm thirty-five.

I lived in a village with my mother and father until I was seven, and I do have brothers and sisters who remain in my village—but the thing was I had a series of dreams. And when I told my parents they knew the dreams were important, and so they told the nearest temple—and it was deemed I had been "called by The Goddess."

I don't see my family much now, and it is hard to remember my early life, but I am so very happy here. This is a life of beauty. A simple life. We try to live harmoniously—with kind words and deeds, and we are gentle with each other, with people, and with animals.

… The temple is on an island.

There are lands nearby, and people get here by boat. This is a well-organized trading and communicating society that operates over huge distances. We have goods from afar, silver and gold and carvings … and this island is sacred to The Goddess. It is a sanctuary, and it doesn't belong to anyone except The Goddess; it is not where people live—except for a few stewards, old men looking after the island, growing food, tending the animals. There are peacocks, gazelles … lots of beautiful animals all wandering about freely, even white peacocks. White animals are especially sacred to The Goddess and they are sent here as gifts.[67]

Ye tells me to go forward in time to an important event.

It is night. I am by the sea. It's where the boats come in, near steps outside the temple. A crescent moon gleams over dark water, and I am standing looking at the moon and basking in deep

---

67 Perhaps this links with the Native American reverence for the birth of a white buffalo. A white buffalo or bison is considered sacred in several Native American religions. They are very rare, but quite a number have been born since AD 2000, and I'd like to think this heralds the return of The Goddess to the world.

feelings of peace. Everything is still, except the serene waters that lap gently against the stone steps. The moon smiles down in her last quarter.

Something on the floor catches my eye. I bend and pick up a broken necklace. A few pearls and beads lie scattered ... the snapping speaks to me of violence—was it snatched? What happened here, has an intruder come ashore? This does not feel right ... ours is a very peaceful community. I turn the necklace over in my hand and examine it more closely. A silver pendant hangs from the broken cord. It is of high value.

I take it to the head priestess.

Ye tells me to go forward in time again.

Daytime ... it's the next day and I am in the same place, watching the boats. I am wondering about the necklace, but everything is peaceful and nothing seems amiss ... it is just another tranquil day. Palm trees and all types of lush vegetation prosper here in our warm, balmy air and in this verdant setting the day is busy with the comings and goings of our many visitors. Another day is unfolding.

I feel so happy.

We are a generous people. We receive gifts from those who come but we give gifts to them also before they leave us. We are thankful and grateful to The Goddess for all that we have been blessed with. We still hold the ancestors' memories of bad times, of cold, of scarcity of food and ages of ice.[68] But this is a time of flowering, a time of plenty when we can grow all we need in abundance. But we do know it could end, and so we shower our thanks on The Goddess for her bounty.

In response to a question from Ye about intruders I reply:

There are no soldiers needed to guard us on our island home because we do not hold on to material things. We do not make ourselves targets by holding on to great wealth. (Only a few special treasures are secretly concealed in the ground.) This conjures an image of our tiny band of old stewards and gardeners with their

---

68 The trading routes were huge and word was carried from land to land, all were connected and all were affected by extreme changes in climate. Not that the ice came to Bahrain, but the world was colder and drier then.

farming implements—they would be our only defense!

Later in the day I find out about the necklace.

It *was* snatched—but by the chubby hands of a child in the arms of its mother. She did not notice the necklace working down through the folds of her clothing, and when it fell to the floor the sound was muffled by all that was going on around her. As soon as she noticed it was gone, word was given to the head priestess.

We mended it for her.

It just stood out as an odd thing that jarred in the intense harmony of our days.

Our days are even and relaxed. We tame the animals on the island, we go swimming, we make things—beautiful things, and we like to help. I help women interpret their dreams. I use herbs to help them incubate dreams that will explain the root of their problems, and I use plants to take ritual journeys to meet The Goddess in search of information on their behalf.[69]

The chief priestess wants us to be happy. We are instruments for The Goddess—that is our role in life, and the happier we are, the more use we are to Her.

There are no male priests on the island, but both priests and priestesses from the temples of the lands around here come for help to unravel a conundrum; when they have a difficult problem we can help them reach The Goddess for deeper insights and explanations.

I like to explore the other worlds, and I do this after purification and fasting. I use plants to create "traveling recipes." We travel with someone, a companion who sits with us but is not on the journey—so they can help us remember what we see, what we learn. They witness, and we do this journeying when we have questions for The Goddess.

This is a good place to do it because The Goddess is close here, on Her sacred isle. This is a nurturing place, and we have a very nurturing view of the world. We see the world as run by a big mother, or perhaps I should say a big "mum." "Mother" sounds colder, more distant, sounds harder to please, more demanding,

---

69 Vision-inducing plants that engender mystical experiences are known as entheogens, "theo" being Greek for God. They were used as part of a ceremony.

judgmental or even punishing or withholding, and that is *not* how we see The Goddess. We have a very optimistic and supportive view of life.

Ye tells me to go to the most important day.

I am fifty-five.

My brother has come to tell me my mother is dying.

He wants me to return with him because my mother wants The Goddess's Blessing before she dies. We can go to see our families whenever we wish, and I tell the head priestess and ask her permission.

I'm given pearls and other gifts for my family, and we go back to the little village that used to be my home. It's not far, about seven days traveling. When we arrive, Father greets us, and all my brothers and sisters gather round. It's good to see them but I'm sad to see Mother so unwell.

I remember her as she was, but now she is old and weak.

Father is not happy because she is ill, and Mother is crying.

They have always been proud that I'm at the temple, and she wanted so much to see me before she died. And now that I'm here she says she can go peacefully, and with The Goddess's Blessing, a special blessing oil for the dying that I have brought with me.

… I'm anointing my mother.

The oil smells beautiful and Father is happy, Mother is happy. There are lots of tears, and gratitude is expressed all around. It is a special, lovely time. Mother dies that night, but it couldn't have been a better end.

We give her back to the earth in a nice simple burial, and the funeral rites are followed by a big feast. At the end of the moon, the Moon of her Return to The Goddess, there will be a final service of thanksgiving for her life, to mark the completion of her journey-time here on Earth and her rebirth into the world of spirit.

As we see it, the moon and The Goddess are entwined.

Our worship of The Goddess is tied in with the moon's cycles, it's as though it is The Goddess's cycles. She is constantly conceiving a new moon and giving birth to a full moon. It's a creative cycle, a "bringing-forth-of-new-life" cycle, and fertility is everything to us. Without it, we perish. There would be no crops, no animals, no children, and no future for us.[70]

I stay to do the thanksgiving, and while I am in the village I meet lots of children, especially the grandchildren in our family. And when the time comes to go, I know I'll miss them. It's been a wonderful family time, very emotional and very bonding. I tell my father to send word if he gets the feeling his days are coming to an end ... and I leave the blessing oil with him, just in case I can't make the journey in time to be with him.

Back at the temple I have time to reflect.

I know my family are happy, and I was happy being with them, but after seeing village life it really makes me appreciate how interesting my own life is here—I'm never bored here ... I have no children of my own, it's true, but I don't mind that—and I've helped bring many others into the world.

But it's not long before my brother comes to take me back to the village again.

I'm brought a message that he's arrived, and I go out to meet him.

I find him standing outside the temple in the sunshine, leaning on his staff. When he sees me he tilts his head to one side and gives me that look of his—a big smile, twinkling eyes, and a quizzical raising of eyebrows that says, "Are you coming, our Ani?"

I take his hands in mine and ask what has brought him.

Father has had an accident.

He had a bad fall and has broken bones in his leg, and now he has a fever.

I bring medicines.

Father gets better once the fever subsides, but although his leg heals, he has difficulty walking.

I enjoy spending time at the village, sitting with him, and talking to the grandchildren as they cluster around us. And at the end of the moon I return to the temple.

Some time later I get word that he died in his sleep.

---

70 Pearls have the luster of the moon, they are round and white like mini moons. They link with The Goddess, and fittingly they are abundant in the seas around Her island. There is something sacred about pearls.

Father has gone …

Ye tells me to go to the last day of that life.

I'm eighty-six, and it's been a long time since I've visited the village. The last time was when my brother, my favorite brother—the one who always came to see me and bring me home—was ill. His health gave way. It was either food poisoning or bad water, but someone else came for me then. I was able to bring him some ease while I was there, but despite my herbal draughts, he died.

And now it's my turn. This is my last day.

I'm in the temple complex as usual.

I'm well, but I'm old.

It's been a full life, with wonderful experiences, and I've learned how to help people. I'm just old and tired now.

That afternoon I go for a lie down. We do not have rooms of our own, just an alcove. There are rows of deep alcoves set along a wall, each housing a wooden chest in which we keep our belongings—our clothing, robes, and any special things we might have. We just sleep on our chest in our alcove, on bedding that is laid out on the top. The walls are painted a warm ochre/pink, and a window aperture above allows moonlight to bathe us as we sleep. The color is cosy and warm, and I fancy I'm in the womb of The Goddess as I drift off to sleep each night.

I make my way to my chest, and lie down. I know I need to rest.

And this is where I die, of old age.

Now my mum, dad, and brother are here … and I'm out of my body, holding their hands. I know it's time to meet The Goddess … I can see the light that brought them … and we move into it. As we ascend in the light we pass through pink, gold, silver, rainbows of colors, and move into golden light. I experience wholeness, connectedness, I feel like I'm dissolving but I'm still me. I feel bliss … I'm home …

But before Ye had let me go up into the light we had done the life review and he had asked me three important questions:

1) What did you learn in that life?

2) Do the people remind you of anyone in your present life?
3) How does it relate to now?

In answer to the first question I had replied:
That happiness lies in helping others.

How simple things can be if you let them. Don't complicate things.

I'd learned a way of being in the world that avoids stress: try just *being*, you don't have to control, force, or shape.

You are taken care of if you are doing what you should be doing.

Keep your wants simple—mental clutter gets in the way of your purpose.

In answer to the second question I replied that the head priestess reminded me a little of my regression teachers, Francesca and Diane; and I recognized my brother to be a friend in this life.

And when it came to the third question, Ye had asked what I'd learned that is relevant to now, to Paulinne, and to the message in the book.

I'd learned about The Goddess. She is a beautiful way to experience the Divine, and this revealed to me how much I'd been brainwashed by the version of God found in the Old Testament— the jealous one, who demanded Abraham kill his son in sacrifice to Him. This version of God is shared by all three Abrahamic religions: Jews, Christians, and Muslims alike.

I'd learned that the Divine archetype needs rebalancing, because the Judeo-Christian-Islamic concept of God as a VERY male being has accentuated mankind's traits for aggression and destruction—which could ultimately lead to the annihilation of our species.[71] (There are echoes of the destruction of Atlantis

---

71 Feminism has sparked research into the earliest texts, and found mention of the feminine Divine. She has been systematically sidelined and buried to tighten the male grip on things—but God is definitely not a "man." When I think about my mystical experiences, I *know* God is not an old man sitting on a cloud. But the use of "He" is so ingrained that I find it difficult to use anything else. But it is not accurate. "It" sounds a bit odd, although accurate, and "She" feels incomplete. God is All That Is, so how could God only be He, and thus, by definition, be incomplete? "They"

here.)

We desperately need the caring, sharing, more giving qualities of The Goddess to be active when business is conducted in the world, that is if we want to leave a world for our children's children. It is unbalanced male energy in the boardroom that is trashing our world, and all for the illusion of short-term gain.[72] The Goddess is the antithesis of destructive greed; it's time more women were in the places of power, it's time to smash the glass ceilings that keep them down.

Today, in a world shadowed and clouded by fear, what will help most is upping the amount of love we give out. Fear is the

---

is tantalizing, except as there is only one Supreme Being it is so obviously wrong. Although don't forget in Genesis (chapter 1, verse 26) there is an example of Divine Plurality where it is written,
"And God said, Let **us** make man in **our** image, after **our** likeness."
"We" would be accurate because at our highest level, at Source, we are all one with God, but it sounds far too arrogant because we are so very definitely not at our highest level down here. When it comes to God, the English language is woefully inadequate, except that it serves to show up the imbalance that has been institutionalized.
The language won't change until our consciousness changes. But there might come a time when "He" sounds strangely archaic and quaint.
(For further reading, historians like Bettany Hughes and Dr. Francesca Stavrakopoulou have researched this and written about how, at the end of the Bronze Age, the Goddess of Wisdom gets edged out by male gods in many cultures; and about Divine Plurality in the Hebrew Bible, where the goddess Asherah was the consort of El, who was later morphed into Yahweh. **Apparently it used to be "Yahweh and Asherah" until She got systematically edited out of the texts, and He was promoted at the hands of male scholars**. So, from the male and female being in balance, we get to the point where we are today with the unbalanced male concept of deity.)
72 And illusion it is turning out to be, especially for the oil companies. In January 2014 the UN climate chief speaking at the Ceres investor event in New York urged global financial institutions to "Beware investing in assets that are already and will soon be losing their value." Because, *"Two thirds of the fossil fuels we have will have to stay in the ground,"* if we are to keep within the carbon budget that will avoid global warming beyond 2C. **Once so valuable, fossil fuels have become "stranded assets."** So why pollute the pristine Arctic and go on recklessly fracking Mother Earth *for just a bit more oil*? It would make much more sense if they used the patents they have bought up and buried over the years—patents on free energy devices and alternative technologies, kept from us to protect their profits. (For more on this read *Miracle in the Void* by Dr. Brian O'Leary, scientist and NASA astronaut.)
Friends of the Earth, Greenpeace and **the Green Party** are all on the side of The Goddess, and on the side of sustainability, compassion and sanity. And if ever there was a time to support them it is now. Greenpeace and F.O.E. are charities well worth supporting. Be a force for change in the world. (Even a tiny direct debit or standing order would be an enormous help.)
Rainbow Warrior, the Greenpeace ship that takes part in environmental protection protests, takes its name from old Native American legends. These speak of a time when the Earth is poisoned and the animals are dying, and they say that it is then that the warriors of the rainbow will come to heal our world and make it green again. (The rainbow in question is made up of all the different colors of the skins of the warriors—people from all nations and races.) Well, no more waiting! This prophecy is already being fulfilled. Be a part of it, be a part of the solution and not a part of the problem.

opposite of love. Fear is the darkness in our hearts that crowds out love and extinguishes its light. Fear and greed are the opposite of what The Goddess stands for.

I can finish the book now! (And it was one book at this stage.)

Ye asks about the necklace. Did it signify anything?
The necklace symbolized a broken thing fixed. Hopes and dreams smashed and repaired ... and it represents the book. Beads had rolled off, and I needed to "restring" the book—put in this new pearl and pull it all together.

And at the start of the session it had been autumn in my place in nature, just as it was in the outer world, where September's Harvest moon had waxed and we were on the way to October's Hunter's moon. It really was a time to hunt out and harvest the knowledge from the past in order to prepare for the coming winter. The next decades will bring many challenges, but if we can find our way through their hard winter energy, there will be a wonderful spring.

* * *

Patriarchy elbowed out The Goddess and sought to legitimize itself by making God male. In meditation once I asked Jesus why he used "heavenly father." He replied that because of the society he was preaching in at the time, no one would have listened if he'd been talking about his heavenly mother!

Women give birth and bring life into the world. Men can declare war and take life, they can kill, but they can't create life. So when they're in control of society, this lack tempts them to try to control women. Patriarchy's fear of women, and the resulting ingrained misogyny, is something that the women of the world have been held back by since then: this is the wound in our collective psyche that needs healing—the diminishing of women and the feminine principle.

But things are changing.

Men and women both have a mix of male and female energies

within their psyches, at about a 60/40 split. While in the past they may have repressed the minority energies, even tried to deny them, men are now integrating their feminine energies, and women are integrating their male energy and reclaiming their rightful place in the world today, as men's equals. Look at how "hands on" new fathers are compared to a generation or two ago. Few men would push a pram in the 1960s because it would have been an affront to their masculinity. Nowadays they push prams and help their partners in every way. They change nappies, wipe away tears, and generally try to be the father their own dad wasn't. It was really only in the 1970s that men started attending the birth of their children, and now it's the norm.

So things *are* changing.

And the energies streaming to us from the universe are changing—because Aquarius cometh—and Aquarius brings the awakening of The Goddess within. The tragedies of the Pegasus years will open our hearts and call forth our inner Goddess. This rebalancing of the energies at the archetypal level in our psyche will result in a more fulfilling way of being in the world for everyone.

- Chapter 10 -
The Extraterrestrial Perspective

By now it was 2017. Time had passed and I still felt we were making progress and that our time line was changing for the better. My original manuscript *Spiritual Gold, Holy Ice, Divine Fire* ended around this point, but it had since turned into three separate books. I'd already submitted the revamped *Spiritual Gold*, and was working on redrafting *Holy Ice* and *Divine Fire* hoping to meet my publisher's criteria. Extra material had benefited books 1 and 2, so I wondered if there was more for book 3.

This meant another visit to the inner world.

As you know, I am no stranger to ET contact, and I know the telltale signs. What looked like a small ball bearing had appeared just under the skin at the first joint of my little finger on my right hand. It raised the skin up and felt hard. I've had these before, they are tracking devices and they usually bed in and cause no trouble—but its presence alerted me to the possibility that I had just had a contact experience. I thought it worth checking out. I didn't know what I'd find, but my hunch was that it might, just possibly, be something important, and that the device had been put there so prominently in order to catch my attention.

It was Monday, 1st day of May 2017.

May Day, the ancient spring festival is a bank holiday, and so Ye was at home and not at work. He offered to regress me. Feeling rather excited and just a bit apprehensive (because I had no way of knowing what the experience would be), I prepared my workroom. I blessed it with incense and lit a candle, then climbed onto the therapy couch, ready to take the familiar shamanic pathway within. I pulled the soft, peach blanket over me and settled back into the pillows while Ye put on soothing music and drew the translucent curtains to adjust the level of light in the room. (Too dark and he can't see to make notes, too light and it's harder for me to visualize). My eyes were closed as the session began.

Ye guided me through a gentle relaxation and some deep breathing, to help me leave the outer world behind and focus within. He asked me to visualize myself in a beautiful place in nature—somewhere I felt relaxed and at peace.

Pictures start coming into my mind at this point.

I see palm trees and shrubs with pink and white flowers, and a white sandy beach, scattered with shells. I tell Ye there are plenty of fish in the sea—that I can hear them laughing!

He doesn't let on this is strange. He asks what season of the year it is.

It's an endless summer here.

But the fish are saying they have breeding seasons—I've never had fish talking to me before! It's a telepathic communication with another life form, and the thought sneaks in that this augurs well for there being an ET contact experience for me to find … that my subconscious knows something, and is already dropping hints about communicating with other life forms …

Ye asks what time of day it is.

Midday, there are strong sun shadows.

Ye tells me to make myself comfortable on the beach.

I lie down on sand near the trees, with the sun soaking into me, and I absorb the beauty and energy of this special place. Then I walk along the beach to meet my guardian angel. I become aware there's a tall winged figure on my right-hand side. But it's not my usual angel, it's bigger. And there's definitely a sense of male energy. He's joking and saying I need a bodyguard for today.

Ye asks his name.

I'm told it's Mimiel, one of Archangel Michael's helpers. He says he has helped me out many times before.

Ye tells me to find a lake, sea, or cave that I will be able to go into and down.

I know the sea is right here, but I want to find a cave.

Mimiel knows where there is a cave … we walk along the beach, turn a corner, and see a cove with cliffs and a cave halfway up. I'm climbing up. The rock is a whitish stone. Standing outside the cave I see little pebbles under foot and sand that's blown here. The cave looks big, but I can see it's darker inside.

Ye asks me to walk in.

It is like a cathedral inside. It's so big.

The floor slopes down toward steps.

Ye asks me to visualize walking down the steps with Mimiel, and he counts from ten to zero.

Now I'm standing on sand, on the cave bed.

Ye tells me to contact the spirit of the cave, the guardian of the inner world.

It takes the form of light this time. There are big comforting shells on the sand. Shells symbolize love and protection for me, and I feel a lovely energy from the shells and a nourishing quartz energy from the sand, which I accept gratefully. I've been stressed!

This was May and I'd been dreadfully worried about finishing books 2 and 3 in time for early June, when Guy Needler was taking them with him to Ozark Mountain Publishing's Transformation Conference in the United States, where he was a speaker.

The angel and the light are laughing. They say, "Don't panic!" And they tell me I will have all the help I need just as I was promised at the start. "Oh, humans do this," they say. "They panic and they feel small, they need to trust themselves more … reach up to the higher levels of their being—they forget who they are, they can do anything if they put their minds to it."

Ye tells me to visualize the guardian of the inner world opening the cave bed. He tells me to float down through it, into my body, to the main area linked to an ET contact experience relevant for the end of the book.

I'm hoping there is one! I hadn't given him anything else to ask for …

But then it happens, and with certainty I know the main area is my hands.

I'm asked what emotion I'm holding there—and it is wonder and excitement, with a bit of fear.

Ye tells me to look at my feet, and to tell him what I see.

My feet are bare. But I see they're in an energy field … I'm in an energy field, in my pyjamas, in space. I can see the darkness of space and little pin-points of stars. I'm in a tube of energy. I'm not alone, there are helper beings with me. They came for me, they brought me here. There's one on each side of me.

It's light inside the tube, but it's transparent and you can see through, can see the darkness of space. We're shooting through it. I feel stationary but I know I'm not. It's a tractor beam. I've seen the beings before, they're from Arcturus. They're small with flat round heads.

Ye asks if I've been taken while asleep—and am I going somewhere?

Yes … It's a good job I don't sleep with nothing on!

I feel excited. I know them, so I wasn't frightened when they came.

I was dreaming, and they came into my dream and took hold of my arms, and then I wasn't dreaming. We left the bedroom in the beam. We went out through the window and the beam was filling the courtyard garden outside the bedroom. It only sucks up what it is tuned to find, so it won't suck up the garden furniture— there would be chaos on the craft where it goes if it did! That's why you have the implants—it only sucks up what it's tuned to find, and it's tuned to the implants.

When did this happen?

This is a very recent experience.

Tell me about the implants.

I mean the little "ball bearing" implants that I've had in my fingers, and toes, over the years. They can be painful till they bed in, but they don't cause any problems when they're there. They may get absorbed by the body given time, it's like a natural decay …

We're traveling but we're getting near something.

We're coming into something now.

I'm on a floor, we've landed inside.

It's more of a space station than a craft—it's big—not like an Earth space station, which is cramped, it's more of a floating city—floating in space … There's a lot of other beings.

The two helpers help me into a suit-thing while I'm still in the carrying tube. They say they don't want any Earth germs up here!

Are there other Earth people?

Not that I can see, yet …

But there is a lot of movement in the periphery of my vision … like beings rushing past who are only partly in the same dimensions as I am.

The suit thing feels silky and flexible, there's a bit of bulk to it, but it's not heavy or uncomfortable, and there is a clear vision panel over my face. There is auditory control, but mainly a telepathic step-er-upper to help me to hear with my mind. It's a transponder.

I can hear the little beings louder now. They are very jolly. They are chuckling as they pull me by the hands along a corridor. I'm aware of movement around me, there's a lot of interdimensional meshing here. The movement is more like shadows passing, but they are all going the same way. They are all pouring into this big briefing chamber. It's really huge. There are tiers of seats—well, accommodation modules to be more precise—there are a lot of helpers of various sorts ordering this, taking the incoming beings to the appropriate accommodation modules. It's like a theater but not.

There are some very big beings here, and very small ones, and a lot of multidimensional meshing so they can come together whatever frequency they exist in. This is a still point in space and time that's been created so this information transfer can happen to a lot of species. And it can be revisited because it is a still point in space and time, a fixed moment in the parallel realities, a special event space, more permanent than the normal ones. This one won't fold in on itself, it's a structural event space in space-time.

Is something big about to happen?

Yes.

This has been orchestrated by some of the higher angelic intelligences, together with some of the ETs that are very highly evolved and are helping with the cosmos. It's about how things work out. Earth's been a bit of a thorn in their side, a bit of a trouble spot, like a naughty child—not the planet, I mean *us*—the problems we've been causing, and the worse problems that we might cause. This meeting isn't just about Earth, we're not that important. But we are one of the items on the agenda.

The little beings are saying I've been here before, and that I've been at these meetings in other places too, that this is just the next one. I've watched these over a period of time because it's part of my mission, that I need to know, because I'm one of the many people who are instrumental in fermenting consciousness, which is why I have been given experiences—and I volunteered for it apparently. It's because I've got a bigger picture of the cosmos and its life forms than a lot of people have, because I've been in a lot of different places in my many lives, and that's why they thought it would be easier for me than for others who haven't had that experience. For a start it's very scary having anything to do with aliens, as well I remember from when I first started to find out about my contact, at the beginning.

There are lots of different types of beings helping other beings here. It depends on what your affinity is—who won't scare you, who will be able to communicate with you, be on your wavelength, on your energy wavelength to some extent. You get matched up, there's a team of helpers that help to orchestrate this contact. It is only when it first happens you feel fear because once you've got a pattern you know what's going to happen, that you'll be safe and looked after. You just feel very tired in the morning when you get back. Because you've really had no rest, even with an astral contact your higher bodies have been working their socks off while you've been asleep.[73]

---

73 An astral contact occurs usually at night while you sleep. Only your astral body is taken to the contact arena, be it a craft, UFO, or whatever dimensional bridging space they are using on that occasion. You simply appear to be sleeping if anyone were to look in your bedroom, but partners are put into a very deep sleep so as not to disturb them before you return.

The chamber is full. The light levels are going down, a huge light appears in the center and the light expands, and it's not just light, it's a substance. It's not like Source where you'd just melt into it, but it's an intelligent mist.

I'm enveloped in this mist of light. It's a subliminal information exchange, a very high-level energy field, on many different levels, that's collecting and collating the information from all the life forms present. It's like a vast computer made of energy mist and light. It's expanded to fill the whole chamber now; everyone is being emptied of their information as appropriate, then it's going to correlate it and give us its findings.

Its findings on "what is." It's a "what-is meter."

(Meaning: what is actually going on at this stage in the evolution of the cosmos, in this neck of the galaxy. *How things are*, the current state of the worlds and of the cultures the beings have been lifted from.) It is calibrated in an energetic sense to ascertain how things are, what is going on in the universe. It's not just about Earth, but about this sector of the universe: the neighboring planets that are connected, the solar system, Sirius, nearby constellations, etc., because they do link, like we have lots of separate cells in our body but each has a knock-on effect on the others, they all link.

This sector is only a small part of the universe, so it's like looking at the health of a small part of the body, a hand, for example, and they take a representative sampling of a smattering of the beings that are there to see what is happening there. (Like you'd take a few cells to check on the hand.) They are asking, "How is the wave of Creation unfolding here?" There's no right or wrong. Just a "what is" and what happens next.

The whole universe is an experiment—not just a game, but *an adventure* for the Creator. And the Creator wants to know how the adventure is progressing, which way it will go. There's no vested interest in the outcome—just "what if." "What if that's happening, what happens next?"

So pow!!! We had the Big Bang. Then it's what's going to happen? How does My energy react with Itself? What does it show Me about Me? That's what the Creator's thinking. So little fragments of the Creator plunge into it, and explore the adventure. That's us and all the beings in Creation. We periodically report back when we die, that's when we have the life review. And we also periodically have this sort of interview session with the levels of overseers of Creation. There are many different levels. We only work with fairly lowly ones where we are, in the human condition, but there are levels and levels above that. It's huge! It's vast!

They're collecting the information, these beings that oversee Creation. We've been called into a local station, that's why this event space is a fixed point; it's admin, Divine admin.

This is stage 1—the collecting of what-is.

There will be a bit of sharing of what-is, we are all valuable parts of it, we get a reward in that we get a share of the information that's been collected. A lot of it wouldn't be appropriate—but some of it is relevant. What I'm going to be given is the what-is from the Watchers. Not the Watchers-and-Catchers of Souls,[74] the Watchers that are Galactic Federation Watchers, the Monitors, the beings that monitor our world and the nearby worlds and the moon.

There's a part of their activity I'm going to be informed about.

Things have to get extremely bad on Earth before we all wake up and do something.

Things will get worse. We're only on the cusp of it. We could make a big difference now but we're very stubborn, and there are a lot of vested interests that want to keep us ignorant—so we don't know the extent of the plotting that's going on, and how serious and precarious the situation is we find ourselves in. There are alien species manipulating it and making it worse, but it is going to get worse because they are exploiting our worst instincts—the greed in us and that sort of thing—not so much on an individual level, but we've been tampered with as a species.

Ye asks if the beings here can help.

---

74 Chapter 10 in *Holy Ice*: They harvest low-vibration souls to be incorporated into their bio-sentient, fifth-dimensional machines to mine minerals. They see us as a resource, like slavers did on Earth.

They don't interfere, they just collect what-is, and see how the adventure is going for the Creator. There isn't a judgment on the outcome. The adventure is in how it happens. We play this adventure without any protection or insurance policies. We are like dodgem car drivers but without the rubber bumpers! (I laugh), or it wouldn't be an adventure, would it? There's not much "health and safety" legislation in a cosmic sense with the adventure! Although there is a bit of help, and that's what angels and guides are for. We do get help from the inner world.

We get help from the planet if only we'd listen. **That's where crystals are important. They hold a lot of information and they tune into information elsewhere even if they don't hold it themselves. And all the crystals in the universe are linked, it's a common thing that happens when gasses combine and the worlds and crystals form. They are not exactly bugging devices implanted into the material world, but they do work with consciousness, and there are higher beings that work through them. They tune planets and can affect the vibration of worlds, and thus of the beings that are on them.** And I can see that the crystal skulls are multidimensional crystals, and that the links into the higher dimensions are stronger with them than with most crystals. **All crystals are part of this massive crystalline matrix that permeates the entire cosmos** but the skulls are like switches or controls. Even if we lost our physical level ones, those that we see, the higher-level ones would still be operating.

But as I know (from previous sessions you will find in *Holy Ice*, chapters 11 and 12), you can forfeit them in the adventure— hence what happened to Mars ... and Jupiter ... and then the fabric of the world degrades ... They are important and that's why it is important that I wrote *Holy Ice*, they are not just to be dismissed as an interesting mystery. They're so much more important than that. They are only a piece in the cosmic jigsaw but their equivalents abound throughout the galaxies. They are obviously not the same shape as ours, but on that same frequency level stretching up through many dimensions.

Somehow they are tied to these event spaces, these permanent still points. The beings can do a what-is check through them if they want, without having to call a big briefing session like this. Because they are resonating with our consciousness, they are picking up an awful lot of information that can be accessed and passed on.

It is coming to me that things are going to get worse.

I'm expecting nuclear bombs to be dropped. North Korea is a possible flash point at the moment—I don't know if it will come to anything or not. I'm not allowed to interfere with the future so I'm not allowed to be given specific things. But Fukushima is still rumbling on. There is a leakage of radioactive material into the environment that will increase and continue, from various sources, some not declared, released undercover as it were. But it will get worse before it gets better. The purpose of this knowledge is to know there is light at the end of the tunnel. We have to hold our courage through the dark times ahead and not give up.

Ye says, like another Dark Age?

Exactly. It will be an eclipse, but when the light comes back there needs to be a few people still here, able and aware, and intelligent because our future will rest with them. I think the Dark Age thing is to do with getting rid of this negative ET influence that's been blighting and manipulating the powerful people, and that is focused on money and great wealth—because while people value it above all else, that's what gives the negative ETs power over them. At the end of the day you can't take your money with you, and the human life span is an eye blink in the journey of your soul. We have been and are still being deliberately manipulated to value wealth and the acquisition of expensive material goods, because it stops you thinking about what's really important. That wouldn't serve the negative ETs agenda.

Though there are a lot more positive ETs, it's a bit like the angels, they can't interfere beyond a certain point because we have free will. Free will abounds throughout the cosmos but it is a particularly strong function of Earth. On Earth you can go further into the dark side with your free will than you do most places.

Ye asks if there is any other information.

Because it is an adventure they're not going to give me too much.

He asks if the contact is regular.

It's regular. I did write about one of these in *Alien Encounters* magazine, (around 1996), where they were assessing our changing level of consciousness as the Awakening began. That was the first time I became aware of the Arcturians, and it was then I met Argle, a Bigfoot who seemed to know me from a previous life. That was a jolly but rather bizarre experience, and the place seemed more localized than this, this is bigger. Though sometimes you just access it on a different level, or perhaps you've learned a bit more and see into the experience a bit deeper.

I'm being told I get taken to other places, that there are other places.

They are always off-world, the places, because they don't want to affect the development of the adventure. You get taken through dimensional bridges to briefing stations. Some of them aren't even in form, like this one is—it's not much higher than our 3D level of frequency—there was an actual floor I walked on, because I wouldn't operate in my Earth form in some of the higher-level places. You get taken to what's appropriate for you if it is a physical not an astral contact.

It's comforting to know that there are higher beings that are doing the admin of Creation, and that there is a purpose to it. But it's not comforting to know you're not going to be saved.

However, it's like when our scientists do lab experiments and give mice diseases like cancers and tumors. They want to see the response when they administer a remedy they are developing. And that's exactly how it is on Earth—the negative ETs came in and the administrators just said, "Well, let's see what happens." They're not going to cut the tumor out or take the ETs away.

Basically, we've been given a spiritual tumor. Whether you call it David Icke's reptilian beings or whatever, we have an ET parasite. It's been leaching us, and it's still doing it, to different extents on different people. It's got a much stronger hold on your psyche when you've got a power and wealth complex. You can see it in people, because when that is all that matters, it's got you. There's a certain amount of natural immunity to the ET parasite in the human race, and Jesus came to give us more, he came to give us a vaccination—by teaching us that love is the only thing that really matters. The vaccination against the ET parasite lies in the truth of his words. In *Spiritual Gold* I have shared the things I heard him say when I was Nadia two thousand years ago. Now I see why they wanted me to write the three books. We needed the important Jesus memories for the vaccination. We needed to understand the crystal skulls because of the crystalline matrix in the cosmos, and how they are one of the factors that are here to help us. They're not the vaccination but they hold the field in the consciousness in which the vaccination can take hold, and this book is to show people what-is and where we are standing, to give them courage through the dark times ahead—because there will be dark times ahead. But we're not to give up because our spirits are so amazing (we only manifest such a tiny part of our capabilities here), but as long as we can just perpetuate our species no matter in how small a way, *eventually* the adventure will come to fruition in a good way. And then we will have achieved the goal humanity was created for.

There doesn't have to be many of us to do that. I don't know what state the world will be in to support us, but thinking we're going to have viable colonies elsewhere, on other worlds—that's just stupid. That might be all right as a lab experiment but it's not part of the Creator's plan. Our DNA has been taken and put on other worlds by higher beings, that's certainly true, but *we* are not going to live there.

It would be like living on a space station forever. In the end, a few generations down the line, you just think "what's the point?" You get nourished on Earth. You're not part of the crystalline matrix if you're in a space station. You could only be there a certain length of time and stay well, and even on another world the crystalline matrix there wouldn't be vibrating in a suitable manner for your cells. You could hold there for a while, but if you stayed forever then you wouldn't be human any more, because you'd be entrained and transformed by the other world's crystals so you would have become something different—not necessarily bad—but different. It wouldn't be the fruition of the humanity experiment, it would be the fruition of whatever that other world's experiment was. It just is. We need to get a grip and get this place (by which I mean Earth) put right.

And it's good we've got the doomsday bunker for seeds,[75] and that there *are* people who are working the right way, there *is* science that is going the right way—but it's a game, and you don't know where it's going, what dice will be shaken next, and that's exciting for the Creator. After all, it's the Creator's game. And we're part of it (and part of the Creator too). The Creator is just tremendous, magnanimous, love and bliss, but It has the overriding need to understand Itself—like we do, and that's why we do, because we are part of the Creator. That's why the Creator goes to all the trouble of Creation.

In the dark times ahead take heart, listen to your heart. If your heart is your compass (Book 1), the map of time shows you how bad things can get (Book 2)—well they can get very much worse than that! The end of Atlantis annihilated that continent and the resulting disturbance to weather and climate made it hard for the rest of the world for a while, but something nuclear could be very, very much worse.

There is a Golden Future, it's how far off it is—that's the debate—and that is what's assessed at the monitoring ... And that's all I'm going to be given for today, but I'll be back for more briefings, I'm being told; but that's enough for now, for this book, now.

So we need to hold on to hope, and live through love (obviously

---

75 The Svalbard Global Seed Vault in Norway was opened in 2008. Built on the island of Svalbard in the Arctic, the storage facility deep inside a mountain is designed to preserve the world's crops from future disasters. Dried and frozen, the seeds of 5,000 crop species from around the world are held there, and it is believed they can be preserved for hundreds of years. So if a nation's seeds are lost as a result of a natural disaster or a man-made catastrophe, the specimens stored in the Arctic could be used to regenerate them.

It was built in the Arctic because it was thought that the permafrost was permanent, but within three weeks of doing this regression, on May 20, 2017, the BBC ran a news story about the permafrost melting. 2016's record world temperatures had seen the access tunnel flooding. The Seed Vault now needs waterproof tunnel walls and drainage ditches outside to take the water away ... a sign of climate change.

being practical and prudent).

Well, there's a lot more still going on around me, but I'm going to be taken away now. The little beings are just pulling me out of the mist.

It's all still going on.

We are a very minor item on their agenda, here on planet Earth.

… And it's out of the chamber and along the corridors for me … but the thought comes that I might be being shown it as corridors just because it's a comforting image for me … It may well not be the ultimate reality of this part of space-time.

I'm taken back to the tube.

The tube is set on reverse, and I'm shooting down it.

I can see the blackness of space and the light of the tube energy.

I'm down above the garden … going in through the window glass—it feels like nothing, slipping through the molecules and atoms of the glass. It's like passing through a fluid, no part of which stays with you, so you don't get wet or anything.

And then some protective thing is taken off me. I left the suit behind before I got in the beam, the silky suit, but I did have something lighter on when I was in the beam.

I'm not actually aware at this point. I am asleep.

They put me horizontally above the bed and then slip me into it. I can see this as I do the recall, as if I'm out of my body watching what happens.

And then they go—out through the window and up the beam.

They like their work, they're happy little souls. (I chuckle.)

Ye asks if we need to do any healing.

No—I was physically protected with the suit, and I wasn't allowed to see things that would disturb me. I feel happier knowing about the experience. The event was just a few days ago, because the implant was put there to alert me to it.

As there's no healing to be done, Ye asks if there is a power animal I need to connect with.

Not a power *animal* but a power *crystal*. Rose quartz links to love, and love is the vaccination. That's when I realize I should put some of our larger pieces of rose quartz under my bed and carry a small polished piece around with me for a while because holding it will nourish me.

Ye asks what color would really strengthen my aura now.

I know it's pink, rose quartz pink, and I visualize my auric field suffusing with beautiful pink energy.

Then it's the return journey.

I float up to my crown and through the open cave bed.

I visualize the cave bed closing and thank the guardian of the inner world for helping us today.

Ye counts from zero to ten.

And I visualize climbing the steps and become aware of being back in the room.

Ye asks what year it is.

2017.

Then I curl up on my left side, and the blanket goes right over me. It is a peaceful few minutes to integrate all that I've learned. When I am ready, I join Ye for coffee.

Then I go to find our rose quartz!

We have a lot on the windowsill of the therapy room, and dotted around the house. I choose a small polished piece that is perfect for my hand, and big raw pieces from the living room I put under the bed. It is good to honor the inner world in the outer world—it is good to ground your vision.

At Mind, Body, Spirit events we like to have heaps of rose quartz on our stand. It looks beautiful and acts like a magnet to draw people. Children are very attracted to it, and Ye and I have given away many a small, polished tumble stone of crystal treasure.

We would learn more about the ET parasite.

- Chapter 11 -
Completion: Session 1, June 2019

The books were accepted. *Spiritual Gold* came out in 2018, and by the summer of 2019 *Holy Ice* was in the final stages of being published. I needed to send in the digital version of the text for book 3 … But something dramatic and undreamed of was happening in the world—Extinction Rebellion had sprung up out of nowhere!

From the first stirrings in 2018, by 2019 it had become a global activist movement of ordinary people demanding action from governments to halt climate change and global warming. In April 2019 cities like London had been disrupted for days on end and people had begun to sit up and take notice. Penguin Books had published XR's handbook *THIS IS NOT A DRILL* (complete with their logo penguin lying dead on the cover!), and more actions were planned in what was to be an ongoing campaign to raise awareness that humankind could no longer ignore the environmental catastrophe unfolding around us.

In August 2018 Greta Thunberg, a Swedish schoolgirl, had started a school strike outside the Swedish Parliament that soon spread all over the world—Fridays For Future inspired millions of pupils to go on strike for our planet. In December 2018 Greta addressed the UN in Poland; in January 2019 she was invited to the World Economic Forum in Davos; she was nominated for a Nobel Peace Prize; and when she addressed the British Parliament in April 2019 they declared a climate emergency. By summer 2019 Penguin Books had published her slim volume, *No One Is Too Small to Make a Difference*. In it:

Greta reminds us that science says we are in the midst of the sixth mass extinction, with up to two hundred species becoming extinct every single day.

And that our scientists have declared that disastrous trends such as erosion of fertile top soil, deforestation of our great forests, toxic air pollution, loss of insects and wildlife, and the acidification of our oceans are just the first few symptoms of climate ecological breakdown.

She says, "I want you to act as you would in a crisis. I want you to act as if our house is on fire. Because it is."

Back in 2007 when I first began working on my manuscript I would never have believed Extinction Rebellion possible. It is a miracle. And Extinction Rebellion was about to come up in an unexpected place.

* * *

It was the last opportunity I would have to add to this book. Ye was retired now, he had much more time, and so we plan a regression—just to check if there is anything extra needing to go in this book, book 3. At this stage, I'm thinking that's the most we will have to do—one session. How little I know!

We begin.

I'm relaxed on the therapy couch in my workroom.

With eyes closed I pass through the initial stages to enter the inner world.

Ye asks me to go to a place in nature, and though it has been two years since the session in the last chapter, I find myself on the same beach again without realizing it. It's a white sandy beach.

I see palm trees to my right, a turquoise sea to my left, and there are bushes and scrubby plants growing in sandy soil behind the trees. Beautiful pink hibiscus flowers grace the bushes. It's pleasantly hot, and I see big shells. I pick up a large conch shell and it immediately starts talking to me. Like the crystal skulls do, silently in my head. It tells me it has a link with the skulls, that it is associated with the Great Temple in Atlantis. It is a conch shell trumpet, it tells me, and it makes the skulls feel happy when they hear it … helps them remember when emperors and kings came to consult with them and their fame was known all over the world.

Well, I wasn't expecting this.

A talking shell. And the crystal skulls rightly belong in *Holy Ice,* not this book.

I have no idea what we are going to find, but when Ye tells me to make myself comfortable on the beach I picture myself lying on the sand, and I'm holding that conch on my chest. It says not to be silly, it's too heavy, to put it down beside me and its energy will be in my aura, making my aura more protective and stronger …

Ye tells me to absorb the beauty and energy I need.

I always enjoy this bit.

Then he tells me to contact my guardian angel.

I look around. She's in the trees … she's looking quite big today. I see wings and a lot of bright light, but I know it's her.

I walk with my angel to find a lake or a cave.

I find a cave in rocks behind the trees. Whitish rocks, hmmm … more of a fine-grained pale gray.

I'm standing outside the cave.

I walk in, looking for the way down.

I see steps. "Carved by those who have gone before you," I'm told.

I visualize walking down (*while Ye counts from ten to zero*).

Now I'm standing on the cave bed at the bottom of the cave … standing on white sand. The steps called to mind the ones that led down from the Great Temple in Atlantis to the natural cave beneath it, where the skulls were kept. Today there were some torches on the walls to help me see my way. Not many, but enough, like in Atlantis. Perhaps it's all the talk about conches and skulls, but I do begin to wonder where I'm going. And this feels like a cross roads; that I could pursue lots of different journeys from here.

Ye tells me to contact the spirit of the cave.

Today it appears as light. It's on my left, while my angel is on my right.

This is the point where I will find out what we're going to do. *He asks the questions I have given him before we started. First off is the big one: Is there actually an experience you need to look at today?*

I know my angel will help me with this, and she says, "Oh, yes!" The conch joins in, it says it didn't come for nothing today, and I have to laugh.

Ye continues:

Do you need to look at a future life?

Or an ET encounter?

Or something else?

The answer from my angel is clear. She says it is "something else" for today, but they will all need to be looked at, because there's more new material than I might be thinking of for book 3. And there's a tie up between books 2 and 3, between the crystal skulls and the future that I'm not aware of. (Though they have been mentioned in *Divine Fire,* it's only been in passing so far.)

Ye: Do you know what that "something else" is?

No! I've got to go further and they'll show me.

Ye counts down from five to zero.

But instead of continuing my journey downward and scanning through my body as usual, I'm pulled to go to the right. I pad along a sandy passageway that leads from where I'm standing on the cave bed toward another cave.

… It *is* the skulls' cave. I recognize it from my past lives.

I step through the cave mouth and enter.

I'm standing on more white sand, but I have stepped back in time.

I see Atlantean priests and thirteen crystal skulls.[76] The skulls are on a high central altar, as they were for my initiation here long ago. The one they called Bah Ha Redo is in the middle, with six skulls to each side. The priests are standing on duty around the walls. Flickering torches light the cave. This is the Holy of Holies beneath the Great Temple of Atlantis, and there is something I'm going to see, hear, or be told that needs to go into *Divine Fire,* that

---

76 That's not all the skulls in the world or even all the skulls the Atlanteans had, just the famous thirteen that were in the capital city of Atlantis, the thirteen that gave rise to the legends.

is needed for the future. I know it's to do with the skulls' mission and their purpose of guiding humanity.

I'm standing here feeling a bit overawed.

My angel is here, the conch in my aura is telling me to get a grip on myself, and to go up the wooden steps that are standing in front of the high altar. I go up, and now I can look down into the skull in the center, which has light coming through it from beneath.

It is apparent I've come for a scrying session.

This is the classic setup.

The conch tells me I don't have to work with all thirteen today, just the one in the middle.

I put my hands around it and introduce myself. (And as I lie on the therapy couch in real life I actually do move my physical hands to cradle the visualized skull in front of me.)

I ask it what I need to know.

I'm told there will be chaos, there will be bad times ahead—tsunamis, famine, political upheaval, governments crashing, and martial law and armies taking control. It's already happening in some countries now—and that is one potential future.

I ask how we can prevent the worst things from happening.

The skull tells me there's no way to prevent them all. It is a necessary cleansing. Like lancing a boil, like how things are better after a storm. We've brought it on ourselves and we all know that really, but the young people, with the Extinction Rebellion, their hearts are in the right place and they need help.

I ask the skull how we can help that surge of intention to manifest, in a physical way.

I'm told we need to listen to them. Change the way we do things, spread the message.

It's too late to avoid everything but it's not too late to be saved.

And not to wait for our leaders to do it, it will be business as usual there. They'll not be rocking any apple carts unless they get made to. It's like the young people are trying to push the apple carts and roll them down the hill because they can see there's no apples in them, they're full of greedy profit-focused entities, corporate entities. There's nothing nourishing in the carts, quite the reverse—and that's when I realize there are living entities that are feeding off the people who work for those corporations, and feeding off the results of their activites … Hmmmm … I can see them!

The skull is showing me big black dragons.

I look closer and see them as very dark gray reptile-wyrm things—wrapped around the planet at the moment, feeding on greed and fear.[77] And we've certainly been putting a lot of energy their way. So those reptile-wyrm things need to go, they need to get their coils off from around Earth. We've got to change the psychic energy that's being pumped out.

It is part of the Extinction Rebellion changes that the skulls want to help with, and it is what spiritual groups who meditate and send healing out to the world are contributing to help with, and native peoples, shamans, anybody who's aware of the higher levels of cause that affect the world of form in which we live.

We've partly created the creatures and we've fed them, but they've come here from somewhere else. Like the Pegasus herds wander through the universe, well, these do too. They feast on planets and when they've killed them and sucked out all the juice they go off and find another one. They are parasites. It's like we've got these massive big fleas, or ticks … Earth's got ticks and we're Earth's brain, but with our thoughts and our activities we've been feeding these ticks. They'll either be the death of us or we'll get rid of them and there will be a resurgence and a Golden Age. How can we get rid of the ticks? We have to feed them stuff they don't like—hope, harmony … love and laughter.

Ye: it's a cleansing.

Yes. And it is part of what the Pegasus beings are here for. They don't like disharmony, and it's disharmony that's been feeding the parasites. So the Pegasus actions are helping to change the harmony balance of the world. We can help that, we need to work with Pegasus … it's quite a disturbing image, these big, dark, wyrm-reptile things.

---

77 Wyrms are a type of dragon in British and Norse mythology that have no arms, legs, or wings. They have the long, scaled body of a serpent.

Ye: I can see them ... writhing.

They've got their claws stuck in. Certain countries give them more of a toehold to stick their claws in. They've got these massive mouths—they're just repulsive. If photos of these made the newspapers ... it wouldn't half wake up the UN and all those people who have conferences about the environment where very little actually happens! We've been looking for asteroids—well, NASA has—looking out for a physical catastrophe but we've got this parasitic one: energy beings, a whole tribe of them having a right old feast. We can't see them, but the ancient crystal skulls can, because being multidimensional their energy flows through all the dimensions, giving them their scrying awareness—they can see and they know. Their job is to alert us, not to do our job for us. Their job is to help us as tools, so we can see what we need to do. That's always been their job—to flag up disasters and give us guidance.

The worlds are platforms for evolution. And our Creator has given us tools to help us as we evolve. We've got nature spirits and angels (the maintenance entities of Creation), and the skulls are part of the maintenance entities of Creation. A consciousness works through them, they have awareness, they have a crystal life force. It bridges from the highest angelic levels down to the actual physical crystal that the consciousness is inhabiting in the form of the skulls.

(I sigh) ... There is no magic bullet.

It is basically an initiation for humanity.

We know we are taking the other species with us into oblivion if we carry on as we are.[78] We've got to actually change, and do things—grow up, open our eyes, and see how we should be responsible for the stewardship of this world—or it will be taken off us, one way or another. Earth would manage just fine without us but we'd be really stumped without Earth. Perhaps a handful of scientists could live on Mars in a bubble of miserableness, but it's never going to be home—nor the moon, nor any other world.

We're too arrogant by half. We have been given a fabulous

---

78 One in four species on the planet is at risk of extinction, according to the BBC News website (7.25.2019).

gift with this world ... we haven't treasured it as we should. But there's time ... but it's definitely "wake up." Wake up before those wyrms suck the life out of us and everything else ... to leave a smoking cinder behind as they go off and look for richer pickings elsewhere.

The solar system used to be different ... there were other worlds. There has been a lot of destruction. The creatures have fed on other worlds and they've come here. Planet Earth is a tasty morsel. They probably couldn't believe their luck when they found it.

Ye asks what advice the skulls can give me to pass on.

We need to find our power. We need to wake up from our dream. Our values need a radical shake-up. We need to focus on what we're leaving our children and our children's children because we've squandered our heritage. And we'll be leaving them nothing unless we start caring for the natural world. You just can't have that nightmare of constant consume and spend, because there comes a point when it ends, when you wake up on a smoking cinder being eaten by a reptile-wyrm. And the reptile-wyrm wants you to hear the siren song of materialism and be heedless, so it can have its full feast.

This is quite unpleasant. I'm not enjoying looking at this ...

There are a lot of people all over the world who have incarnated to bring a shift. The young people have come. They are warriors. They have come from difficult times in the past, they are great souls—I'm getting tingles down my legs as I access this—great souls who have incarnated here to lead a revolution in a planetary sense. A revolution about how we open our eyes and perceive the world, and our responsibilities in that world. The world is our family and we have to love our family—the creatures, the rocks, the air, and the water. They are all alive. They have consciousness on different levels. They are our family and we need to love our family and take care of it. Not piss all over it—it's just horrible what we've been doing.

There's a tremendous innocence with animals ... butterflies, and plants ... they're gentle and innocent—and we aren't. We do have those qualities but they have been undervalued. The whole "woman thing" in society—the caring roles—they've been undervalued. They don't even figure in GDP and things like that. We've had a completely wrong head on our shoulders when looking at values and value systems ...

Well, it's wake up now or we've had it.

We'll die in our sleep if we don't wake up now.

We know this, but have we changed? The young people know this. Perhaps there's no hope for the old people in power. Perhaps they have to be removed from power and not voted for. If everybody voted green and took a huge interest in green issues we could do marvelous, magical things.

We all have the magician archetype within our psyche, and it hasn't been honored. It's in bad shape. We need to re-enchant the world. That's why people are depressed—they've lost their magician archetype. Their lives need re-enchanting.[79] How can you re-enchant your life if you're living in a concrete box in a miserable urban desert? When the bees are dead and the trees are struggling ... And that's why so many of us are on antidepressants.

That alone shows things aren't right.

It's a barometer that shows how we are wrong, how we are adrift, how things need to change. Education needs to change. The stress-inducing tests we subject our children to are measuring the wrong things. Children need to do wilderness training, they need to grow plants. Every school should have fields and wild areas and gardens. Schools should do beekeeping and make a profound study of insects and their wonder, and look at the clouds and the weather—that needs to be taught to everybody—about the water table and geology ... and there's so many things on the curriculum today that are irrelevant and unnecessary. And all the important things that feed the soul and the spirit, and the psyche—that keep people happy and well balanced—aren't there because the way we measure things is all wrong. Those wrong things have brought the world to the pretty pass it's in now.

Ye: Any advice from the skulls?

---

79 That is why the Harry Potter books and films are so popular.

Yes, people know that message is right. They feel it. The young people know it. We need to trust and honor our young people. We need to spread their message. (I'm getting tingles down my legs again.) Our young people have come to save us from ourselves. There's an epidemic of suicides in their generation because it's such a bloody hard job because we're so stuck. We have to let them do their work, the work they have come to do, let them complete their missions, otherwise we all lose and there is no future. The generations yet unborn will be forever unborn if we get it wrong—and we have to carry that if that happens. We're all responsible for that.

Every single one of us on the planet, no matter how rich, will have to face the Creator when we die. We will have to look at our soul, we will have to look at our spiritual attainment, because there is no escape. When you die here you leave this level and you go into the higher levels and then you have a reckoning. All the religions in the world have always told us that, but people think they can cheat their way out! (I laugh.) We are droplets of the Creator and you can't cheat yourself. There really is no escape and the values on the higher levels are so different from this level that you wouldn't want to cheat yourself.

There's no escape. You take the right path or there's a reckoning. The cosmic responsibility of losing the future for your species is huge. You won't just disappear with a "puff!" and it's over. Death is not the end of it. The reckoning will take you into your next cycle of incarnations … for the lessons to be hammered home.

I'm finding this hard. I'm hoping this is enough …

The conch and the skulls say, "You've got it." They tell me there is an audience out there for the books—the warriors who have come—and that the books are riding a tide, that I can see it in the way things have happened, and the tide will take them forward to the right people.

It had been a powerful scrying session and I was glad it was over.

The skull I have been gazing into tells me the other twelve

skulls were present to boost the energy, because it took their combined power to show me those wyrms, the other-dimensional reptilian "ticks."

I need to thank the skulls.

I visualize putting my hands on each one and say, "Thank you and bless you." And then it's "Thank you" to the Atlantean priests—because we have come back in time for this. I'm told it was granted because I had been a priest, I was one of them, and I'd done my duty in this place when I was Arlos.

I feel rather overawed, a bit overwhelmed.

I come back down the wooden steps in front of the altar table.

I'm being given a drink of crystal water by the priests to restore me. (That is what they call their healing water when quartz crystals have marinated in it. There is no physical drink, but in real life I swallow several times.)

Ye: Who were you in that experience, what was your name?

I was me now, because I had the knowledge of my books, but I was also keying into who I'd been; the thread that was Arlos was very active. (We are all like ropes of many colored threads, if you will, and each thread is one of our other incarnations. Some threads are very much on the surface, they are very active, others are hidden in your core, in your heart and you are less aware of them. The rope shimmers. It is not static. The threads move as we face the challenges in our life, and need to draw on the strengths or skills of our different incarnations.)

Who was I? I'm me but I'm more than me. I'm all the "me's" I've ever been.

I'm Arlos-me, Pegasus-me, a warrior-me, Akbar-me who Death showed the elemental dragon-wyrms to when they first arrived. I'm the "me" who once knew Merlin—there's a big tie-up here with the Merlin chapters in *Holy Ice* ... *I'm even future "me's"* ... (At this point time had dissolved, collapsed in on itself. The past, future, and present were all interpenetrating the same moment. And that's the power of the skulls. They had drawn me back in time, to a time when the thirteen were together in their place of power, amplified by the energy in the crystal-rich rocks of Atlantis. Then they accessed the future for me to see a present danger. To raise my power of perception they collapsed time so I could draw on many of my other incarnations' skills and power in the same moment.)

That was mind-blowing …

Ye asks me the purpose of the crystal water.

It was to help solidify the skulls' energy and the mission within me. It was given with the very highest of intentions. The priests were doing what they were told to do by the skull Bah Ha Redo, as they called it. The skulls transcend time and … they're not exactly in charge, but they hold the plans for the beginning and the end of the universe, and they give good advice and very sound counsel.

Ye asks me if there is any healing I need to do.

Yes. We need to release something with the rattles … ugh— ugly dark gray reptile-wyrm energy. I am holding it in my heart, in my body, in my aura. Where did I get it from? Perhaps I don't want to know …

*Ye: We must all have atoms of it in ourselves (*Me: yes … *) and then together they become the wyrm that's around Earth.*

You're right!

Ye: We all have atoms of it—oh God, I'm tingling—and they all link together to make one that's …

You're right—we're all like cells in its body. Like we're cells in God's body, because we're little holograms of everything … yes …

Ye uses sounds and rattles to help me release the horrible dark gray energy and give it to the angels …

Flipping heck, that was grim. It was smoking and smelling of acid.

Ye asks what color energy I need to heal and rebalance with.

Multicolored iridescent golden sparkles, and pink for the heart and the body.

Then we ask the Archangels who underpin our inner world work, that's Michael, Uriel, Gabriel, and Raphael, if they would take some of the reptile-wyrm energy away from the world in order to help the Extinction Rebellion energy come in. They do, and I see them get the Pegasus herd to round up more, and drive them into the heart of the sun, toward the pathways of light that go back to the Creator.

The sun is enormous; there are so many angels there in higher dimensions that they will be able to help the wyrms complete their evolution on a much higher plane somewhere else. It will be a win/win for the wyrms. We created them as much as anything, so we are responsible for them; they are not just "other" and bad. The life forms in the universe have created them, and we're part of the family of life forms in the universe. And we've actually fed them, and so we've created a lot of them ourselves. At first there were only one or two that came, but we helped them to breed, I mean our dark side did, by our base actions—by our greed and lust for power, the dark side of the human psyche.

I laugh—I think we need a moment to balance here! For us, for the sun, and for Earth.

Then I visualize healing energy coming in, to fill the place where the wyrms had been around Earth, and to make it uncomfortable for those that are left—beautiful sun energy flowing in and around, beautiful angelic energy—especially Archangel Michael's energy because his is blue. And the Earth is blue. Beautiful blue Michael energy flowing around Earth, strengthening her whole auric field and raising her vibrations to help the planetary shift that's going on. And love energy from Archangel Gabriel and healing energy from Archangel Raphael and truth from Archangel Uriel—because the truth of what mankind has done needs to be understood and owned, then we can move into our power to put things right.

So it's all their energies now flowing in and around the world, flowing down into the clouds, falling as rain, into the water, into the seas, onto the land, into the plants that are growing, into the plants that the animals are eating, that the birds are eating, that the insects are eating, into the water that we're drinking, and into the food that we're eating.

May scales fall from our eyes so we see the truth. May love make our hearts swell and give us the push to be kind to the world and the life forms in it. May we express healing into the world, just through our footsteps as we walk about, through the words that we say, through the breath we exhale, through our thoughts, through the energies we emit, that through our energy emanations we may bring healing and be a blessing to the world and to God's creatures. And we ask Archangel Michael to give us our power and our swords of truth.

Unbeknown to me, Ye has picked up the biggest of our conch shell trumpets, and he blows it.

That was a surprise, but it was inspired.

I can tell the conch loved it, the skulls loved it, and the wyrms didn't like it. (I have to laugh.) I am told conch sound is very grounding for Earth and strengthening. Conch shells are from the kingdoms of the sea and the sea gave us all life.

I say, "Thank you" and "It is done."

I turn to leave. I see the back wall of the cave. It has been carved to resemble a huge skull face and I have to step into the dark shadows of its mouth to reach the passageway beyond. I pad along the passageway … back to the white sand at the bottom of the steps.

Ye counts me up the steps from zero to ten.

And I'm back in the workroom and in present time.

Ye asks me what year it is.

Saturday, the 8th of June, 2019.

I roll onto my left side and curl up. The blanket goes over me and I retreat into this womb-like space, to be reborn into my new understanding. This is always how we end, whatever the session, but it feels incredibly appropriate today.

Ye goes to make us some much-needed coffee.

And we know we have two more sessions to do.

- Chapter 12 -
Completion: Session 2, July 7, 2019,
AD 2300 to AD 2400+

It is time for the next session.

I go to the place in nature and it's the same beach again, the palm trees and the turquoise sea are waiting for me. I sit looking out at the waves. This time it is sunset, the sun is creating golden patterns on the water—hinting that day's end means the end of the work for the books—that the golden path of the sun is taking me toward completion. It is a warm balmy evening, beautiful and peaceful … I hear the hypnotic rhythm of the waves. I absorb beauty and energy, the power of the sea, the warmth of the land, the freshness of the air.

Ye tells me to contact my guardian angel.

She comes up behind me. Helena is wearing white and she's bigger than me today. Sometimes she's quite small. She says it's because she has a big job to do—we're going into the future. The future isn't yet set. She's going to have to wrap her wings around me tightly so I don't interfere with it.

We walk down the beach a little way and then head inland, to the cave. All the sessions beginning with this beach are linked, even the next will start the same way.

The cave is in gray rock today. Gray sandstone.

I walk into the cave … looking for the way down. I'm walking over sand which has little shells in it, and it crosses my mind that a big wave must have come in since I was last here, to wash shells so far from the beach.

I find the steps and go down.

Ye counts down from ten to zero.

I step off, onto the cave bed. Again I'm standing on sand.

Ye tells me to contact the guardian of the inner world.

Poseidon comes. He is wearing a crown and has his trident. He looks very jolly, which is a relief, because he has another aspect (as Atlantis discovered to her cost). He is laughing, and says, "I thought you'd come." (We have a bit of history, Poseidon and I, from the end days of Atlantis, in book 2.)

Ye tells me to visualize Poseidon opening the cave bed, then counts from five to zero as I visualize myself floating down through it, down into my own body through my crown, and going to the main area in my body linked to the experience I need to see now. Ye asks which area I'm focused in, and what emotion is linked to the experience.

It's my feet … I'm wanting to run. There's fear there too, fear of what I'm running from.

Ye tells me to sink into the emotions and let a picture come clear, and to look at my feet and tell him what I see.

I see bare feet on a beach … but I am wearing clothes, white leggings and a simple top made of a natural vegetable fiber, like bamboo. The fabric is absorbent, comfortable, and cool. It's a very practical garment, easily washed. We all wear the same, it's not a uniform as such because we ornament our tops, embroider them, stitch on tiny shells, that kind of thing … they're just the easiest clothes to manufacture. They are standard issue, sent to us from a central headquarters.

Ye asks me if I'm on my own, or if anyone is with me.

I'm alone, I've been sent out as part of my job. To beachcomb. I'm looking for things the sea has brought up.

Manufacturing is difficult for us and we don't do much of it now. There aren't many people on the planet, but there's still plenty of stuff from the past that washes up. Some things may actually be useful, other stuff is a great curiosity, and at the very least we incorporate it into our big wall mosaics and the sculptures we make.

We have a sculpture park. It's a tombstone to what was.

All sorts of bits of rubbish and flotsam and jetsam are put to a new use and turned into art. It is a lovely park, stretching inland from here, filled with wildflowers and plants and trees, dotted around with these strange sculptures we make from the gifts of the past that the sea brings us. It covers valleys and hills, mountains. It is a huge wild area. We don't know all the sculptures that are there.

Ye comments—there's time for art?

Oh, we have plenty of time for art.

There's a tiny bit of manufacturing that happens at a central location—well, to be accurate at several locations, dotted around the country, but it doesn't involve us. We grow our own food, some in soil, and some in a laboratory setting with hydroponics— plants having their roots in nutrient-enriched water to feed them. We don't really eat meat now because it's far too intensive to raise. We get protein from vegetables, by eating beans and lentils.

Ye asks me how far this is in the future.

Three hundred years … a long time. Humankind is still on Earth, but there are not many of us. We live in a stable society that's been going on for generations. It's an ordered world. Very peaceful, there are no wars. There aren't enough of us for wars. Anyway, there's no need for wars because we share the resources we have, we barter and trade. We need cooperation from other communities or we'd never get anything done. This is a time of self-sustainable, isolated units of population with a centralized network of communication and supply. And this pattern is more or less duplicated in the different countries and landmasses of the world. Obviously, it varies a bit here and there, but cooperation enables supply, and that enables a decent life. We know we'll eat—bar natural disasters like asteroids or volcanic activity …

Ye asks what country I'm in.

Scotland, on the west coast of Britain, the Atlantic coast.

But it's warmer than in Paulinne's day.

I'm on a beach. I live here. I'm looking for things that might be useful … even if just for the mosaics in my rooms, or perhaps to stitch on my clothing, because we are always encouraged to express our unique individual tastes. We are given a "blank canvas" of an outfit and we customize it. Some dye their clothes. This is looked upon with favor. Imagination is valued here. It never was in the old days … when the imaginative people were just used by the system, by big business, and they were never truly valued, just exploited—but there's been a massive shift.

Because there's so few of us we celebrate individual talent.

There isn't the search for ever-expanding markets/money/big manufacturing/greed process anymore. The arts aren't exactly our currency but the arts are what we value. No one has lots of money in a bank now because we don't really use money. Or have banks. It's bartering and exchange now. The artists, the poets, and the dreamers are very valued—they are the high-ranking levels of society.

We value beauty—of words, and actions—and storytelling. Just like in the very ancient times when people gathered around a fire in the evenings and told myths and legends, we have times in the evenings where we come together and share poems or things we've written.

It's a lovely life, it makes us happy.

We all have a turn growing things, and that makes us happy too. And you can have pet plants, you know, when you just grow things for beauty—it's not all utilitarian.

Ye comments that it sounds like Utopia.

Yes … but it's not too easy, otherwise there'd be no sense of struggle, achievement, and purpose. But there's not much struggle. You simply have to pull your weight with the community activities to make sure we've got food and necessary things, but there's plenty of leisure time beside that.

Ye asks what maintains the population—what stops the population expanding?

We've lost our fertility. Babies are rare. They are celebrated events. No … the Paulinne times put too much poison into the soil and the air. And later we found out it was deliberately orchestrated, what with the stuff that was sprayed on the crops and chemtrails and things. Well, there were too many people but if you go too far the other way there's not enough. There's an equilibrium now.

Ye asks about technology.

It shifted. It didn't stop developing, so the technological revolution that came out of the industrial revolution continued. It wasn't very polluting and didn't need vast amounts of power in the same way as the old-fashioned factories did, and it was very valuable. So we still have satellites—monitoring systems—so we have good communications with other countries and everybody can see what everybody else is up to, so there are fewer secrets in the world and less need for them.

We do get together, we do travel.

Hmmmm … how do we travel? … Teleporting devices, they open a dimensional worm hole and you re-coalesce on the other side. It is a bit scary, but we've been doing it for a long time and there don't seem to be any ill effects. You know how you astral travel when you dream at night? It's like that—you don't take your body. You astral travel then re-animate a receptacle vehicle. You leave your body in stasis and astral travel. You go to a place to do this, and at the place you arrive there's amorphous forms awaiting you. You pop into one of those and your energy customizes it so it wears your face. It's not quite as solid as you, but it is you, and you keep the memories and experiences that you gain when you're in that form … It's a form you inhabit.

Ye asks my name.

Arwinn, I'm female. They say women have more patience at beachcombing, but that doesn't mean men aren't good at it. And men have more strength to move big things and bring them back. Beachcombing is one of our favorite activities. You need exercise, and beachcombing means you are walking and getting exercise and fresh air at the same time, and then there's always the thrill of the hunt—what you might find. In the twentieth century, people went shopping, and in ancient times people went hunting. Humankind has a restless spirit and always wants to know what's around the corner … because you never know what little treasures from the past you might find. Perhaps plastic trinkets. We don't make plastic anymore. That got banned.

Ye asks what I found.

I found some ring pulls. I like those. They've got little holes in them and they're easy to string up. And some sea glass—there's never much of that unless it's after a big storm.

Ye tells me to go forward in time.

I'm in the place where we live.

It's the communal evening. We've eaten. We eat a lot of soups and stews with seaweed in it—there are a lot of beneficial minerals in seaweed. There's also a bit of radiation but by now we cope with that. A lot of nuclear reactors went under the sea when the sea levels rose—but what can you do?

The meal is being cleared away now …

And then it is community time—we all like this.

In olden days they'd have gathered around a fire but we don't need to do that, we have renewable solar heating and tidal power. It is the only sensible thing to do, it's so easy and the technology for these things got much better. We laugh when we look back at the twentieth and nineteenth centuries—so primitive. And so avoidable if all those patents hadn't been bought up and buried in vaults by people with vested interests in the fossil fuel industry. It was a scandal, and it came out later.

Ye asks what we are doing in community time.

It's broadcast time—we're watching our friends in other places.

We sit around a circular screen. A projection energy beam comes up from the middle of the floor and the pictures are on that. I think lasers are involved, and it's like a hologram. We can all see it from wherever we are.

First the news from around the world. We need to know what's going on in a planetary sense about active volcanoes or whether anybody has spotted an asteroid—certainly about any plagues— or weather problems that might be coming our way. And there's good news as well—when people have discovered things or new ways to do things. There's always a feel-good element to the news toward the end. The news is always interesting, and afterward there's entertainment.

We have music.

We have musical instruments that we've invented, ways to use sound and voice that are really beautiful—harmonies that smooth out your energies and have a healing aspect, like harp music has always had a healing aspect, because it vibrates the water in the cells of your body and brings harmony. We developed this concept further, and we add wind and sea noises as well. It's quite beautiful. So it's a healing time but it is also a dreaming time.

In Paulinne's day people took drugs, but we go on journeys with this music. It changes our brain rhythms. People used to take Ayuhuasca and drugs to have experiences; well, you don't need to do that now, you just need to listen to the music and it changes your brain patterns and takes you into the inner world.

Even children in our schools learn about inner guides and power animals and the shamanic side of life, because that gives life its meaning and enchantment. The ancient peoples and the indigenous peoples knew the power of those things, but with what followed from the Age of Reason in eighteenth-century Europe, these things were laughed at and not understood, and it was a great loss, but now they've come back.

So it's our dream time now.

We might meet plant spirits, or travel to other worlds, we might go into our memories of past lives. Oooh … all sorts of things … People write poems and stories about their experiences sometimes, and later they hold readings. It could even be broadcast. There's a huge archive of past life memories that are drawn on for history lessons in our schools; if a culture doesn't have its history it hasn't got anything. It doesn't know where it's come from, doesn't know its roots, so it's lost. That's important.

Ye sums up: it's a recharging and information gathering time …

Yes … it heals the body, instructs the mind, and heals the soul and spirit, it enriches. Oh, we see life so differently now (to Paulinne's day). It's not the struggle it was for the very early people many centuries ago. And it's not the desert of meaning that the twentieth and twenty-first century suffered from—which caused epidemics of depression, alienation, unhappiness, and drug abuse. That desert of meaning has been watered and become verdant with meaning now.

Things are so different.

We are ready to meet the brothers and sisters in the stars now because we're not the destructive, primitive creatures we used to be. We really have changed. The old "Homo Brutalis" types only crop up occasionally today, and then those people get put into an intensive program, including physically stimulating various brain centers to evolve them a little.

Mmm ... so do we meet the brothers from the stars?

Ye: Yes, do you meet the brothers from the stars? Physically meet them?

It's more astrally, like when we travel on Earth, we can also travel to other worlds. There's not a great deal of contact but there is a bit. We mainly travel to their ships that circle Earth—there's still mother craft orbiting that monitor us—but we know about them now, and we have friends on the craft.

We have been welcomed into the galactic family.

We had a little help from them with the technology side of things...

Ye says everything sounds ideal.

Well, at the human level you could say it was ideal. You can express your individuality, and there's a very benign welfare-organization-type-of-system that looks after you. But there are still the vagaries of the planet to worry us; the planet got very destabilized in the bad times. In the twentieth and twenty-first centuries, as well as the poisons sprayed on crops and the land, far too much radioactive rubbish was generated and spread around. There was irresponsible behavior with that level of things, which resulted in magma systems deep in the earth getting destabilized, and volcanic activity increasing, generating frequent tsunamis ...

Ye asks if I live near the sea.

Right by it. Not all our settlements are on the coast, some

are inland. But the sea is a rich place for food. There are little crustaceans, sea limpet things, seaweed, and we farm fish in the sea. That's the nearest we get to eating meat—the soft flesh of sea creatures. Even that's a treat we don't have every day. We eat plenty of seaweed though. It's the basis of a lot of things. It helps us grow strong because it's mineral rich, so we're healthy. But there are few wild fish in the sea anymore.

Ye asks me to describe my home.

I live in a white, smooth, circular structure that's low to the ground, wide at the base, and comes up to a slim tower in the center that gives vision over a distance. The tower's main use is to see tsunamis coming, as these are a frequent event. The round base is designed for tsunamis to flow safely over, and that's where we live. The thin tower is greatly reinforced and is designed to part the tsunami water like a knife. It has a sharp edge running up and down the side facing out to the waves. Before we came up with this design there was a lot of damage done to buildings. We had to learn better ways to build because we expect tsunamis now. You have to be careful when you're beachcombing of course, but it has been quiet for a while.

We sleep in our own individual units, we have our own rooms. We have a private life and a community life, we have friendships. There's less of the nuclear family set-up, and relationships are more open, but you still get pair-bonding because that is the most successful formula for happiness. But if you don't meet someone you want to pair-bond with you might have a succession of relationships. All that "morality" stuff has gone. You do what makes you happy, but pair-bonding generates the most happiness for most people.

Ye asks if there is anything else I need to see.

I glimpsed this life in a workshop I did twenty years ago with Dick Sutphen. I saw the structure where I live, and saw myself beachcombing, and I saw what happens next—a tsunami wave comes in. I saw myself racing back to the structure, which is why my feet wanted to run at the start of the session, but I'm not sure of the outcome. In one scenario I got back and the door shut behind me and I was safe, in another the wave took me. It was like two equally weighted moments in time, both balancing in scales. Which one will weigh down and manifest had not been decided. So I'm not sure what's going to happen now, not sure which way the energy will flow. And I'd like to look into that.

I stare out at the sea.

If I look hard I can see the tsunami on the horizon, it's suspiciously small but it is rolling in. Something has happened somewhere on the seabed that's generated this rogue wave. It doesn't look like much at first. But I've seen it now and it's racing toward me. I'm running for home. I'm running pell-mell through the sand. Sand isn't the fastest thing to run on when you've got bare feet. The wave is beginning to rear up—but I'm nearly there! Someone is holding the door open for me because they know I'm out … ooooh … I throw myself through. I'm lying on the doormat gasping.

I'm in through the door and it has closed behind me.

I hear the bang as the water hits. But I'm all right, I'm inside … I'm (coughing) panting, breathless.

I'm glad I accessed this time line because I died in the other one. You know, it's because I looked at this future life in my present life (as Paulinne), that my intuition was sharper when it happened. If I hadn't done the inner work with Dick Sutphen and with you now, that wave would have got me. It was a sneaky one. It was big enough to kill me but it wasn't big enough to be seen by satellites until it hit. We got no warning on this one. We have to live with this on a daily basis. Thank goodness, the watchers in the tower saw it and had the door open for me—or I'd have had it!

I desperately needed something to drink.

Something to eat.

And a rest in my room … The tsunami covered our building. We have windows, we can see it. The water pressure's tremendous. It'll bring some interesting beachcombing things up … they threw all sorts into the sea back then … And a lot of fish and seabirds just choked on plastic and died and couldn't reproduce … there's a few fish left, and we farm fish. We like birds too. We have tame birds. In fact, we like creatures—because it's quite lonely on the planet without our fellow creatures and there aren't many these days.

They rewrote the Bible. Took out that bit about how we have dominion over the beasts and everything and put in a more accurate translation about how we were to be stewards of the world, like shepherds and farmers. We were supposed to look after and nourish and protect … there were a lot of revisions to correct distortions that had crept in.[80]

Hmmmm … especially about God being "He." … Laughable now, but very sad, the results of mistranslations and deliberate alterations, omissions, and … well—it's the sins of the past. The sins of the fathers brought misery, the sins of the fathers were visited upon their children. That's long gone. Generations of female scholars who were interested in the original texts went back to the very oldest manuscripts, parchments, and records—and there were more archaeological finds too, that were assessed and translated by women. Because women never used to have those jobs. So that's a good thing that came in the twenty-first century, women's education got a lot better, and that brought a massive balance back into everything and a re-looking at the past, and at beliefs and religions.

Because all the religious teachers came with good hearts and a good message, but in the search for power some of their later followers twisted things, mistranslated things, and deliberately misinterpreted things and cut things out.

Ye asks if there is a role for religion in this (future) society.

We still have the Bible. And we keep the archaic forms of all the holy books. It's one of the subjects we teach the young ones—our spiritual history, but we have a much purer form of it now. We still have mystics and seers, and when we do the journeying at night people meet angels and God … it's not an educated priesthood and then just the ordinary people who have to take

80 It is in the first book of the Old Testament, in the very first chapter, Genesis 1:26. "And God said, Let us make man in our image, after our likeness: and let them have dominion over the fish of the sea, and over the fowl of the air, and over the cattle, and over all the earth, and over every creeping thing that creepeth upon the earth."

Notice it is "us" and not just "he" for God. That is how the Bible starts off. Then it changes.

their word for it. Everybody is their own priest or shaman now, everybody is trained and enabled to get their own higher wisdom and to communicate with their own higher self and their spiritual levels of being. We are not as blocked and isolated and stuck in our three-dimensional body as we used to be.

We're aware that we are multidimensional. And that our spiritual bodies transcend time. We have a much better understanding of these things now—which is why we're all happier, and have more harmony. Because the truth is the truth, and we can access the truth ourselves directly now, we don't have to take somebody else's word for it.

Organized religion changed greatly.

But people are still called to be teachers of spiritual matters.

Ye says it's broader ...

Yes. It's so different. Spiritual teachers encourage people to check what they are saying for themselves, it's about empowerment and the individual person having their own experiences, which is something Paulinne was into in the Paulinne life—with her enlightenment experience and loving inner work with guides and angels.[81]

It's much more mainstream now.

Ye says the value of your work survived.

Yes. And that's my concern now—passing it on. Teaching people how to do shamanic inner working and that's why I've written the books, because the books carry the message. It would be nice to leave people trained. But of course it's not just me. Think of all the good work Dick Sutphen has done and is doing, and the amazing legacy Dolores Cannon has left the world. And even if it's simply people reading the books and getting ideas and going off on their own pathways—that's what's important, to know that there is more. I was born knowing there was more and being hungry for it.

Seeing this life makes me happy.

It validates what I held dear, the work that I did when I was Paulinne, and shows that we do have a "coming of age" time as

---

81 Covered in *Spiritual Gold*.

a species. We have passed tests and cleared hurdles, and we have moved into a different way of thinking about ourselves and our place in the universe, and our place on this planet, and we have achieved a point where we can be welcomed into the cosmic brotherhood. High five for us! This makes me happy.

Take me to the last day as Arwinn now …

… I'm old, 140. We live longer because life isn't as physically taxing as it used to be, and even though there's that toxic/poison/radiation thing still going on, which we inherited from past generations, we know a lot more about the human body and a lot more about healing. The harmony music/dreaming at night heals on all levels and the body can repair better.

People do die earlier than this because of bodily weaknesses like a weak heart, but generally people live a lot longer and with better health. We don't need pills and tablets and wheelchairs and things. The shamanic dreaming and healing really works—that, and communicating with the Higher Self, but there does come a time when it's time to go.

Like now, it's my last day.

It's the afternoon and I'm in my room. The walls are richly covered in mosaics I've made and I have a very comfortable resting place, a soft spongy mattress that gently supports me, with nice light covers of a soft, silky vegetable material. Mmm … it's a nice place to be and my friends are here. I have young friends as well as friends of my own age, and I want to say goodbye to everyone.

I just feel very tired and I know it's time to go. I had an experience last night in the healing session, in the journeying. My angels and guides came and said it was time, and I thought, yeah, they're right. They said there was something exciting for me to do next.

Ye laughs.

That got me a bit curious.

I think I'll journey tonight but not come back to my body … that's very often how it works. You meet the angels and guides and they take you on into the levels of light and then … what do we do with the bodies we leave behind?

Hmmm … We don't bury them. Recycling of the flesh for a protein soup, that's what happens … because we don't waste anything. It would be done in a very respectful way, and not for several days because the subtle bodies detach over time. They don't just detach in one go. We understand these things. We leave the cells of our body as a gift to the community, even our bones. We're happy to do that, as a "thank you" for the life we've had. It does make sense. You could be buried in the ocean but the fish would eat you, buried in the ground the worms would eat you, to be burned would be polluting and waste trees.

Ye: How old were you when you escaped the tsunami?

In my twenties. I was young and careless, but with strong young legs!

I haven't had the energy to go out beachcombing for a while. I've been sitting in the sculpture garden that's just behind our home and talking to the birds there and it's been nice.

Ye: What did you learn in that life?

The value of beauty. Most of my life was concerned with creating beauty, in the sculpture park, and I did murals for other people in their rooms, with the things I found, and incorporating things they'd found. I'd ask what sort of mural they wanted, what the feeling was they wanted created. I enjoyed that. I even went into other communities doing murals for people, so I had a bit of a name for myself. It was a good life looking back.

Ye: Lots of creativity and lots of beauty.

Oh, and I loved the evenings with the astral traveling. And you didn't have to worry where your next meal was coming from. That's why I lived so long. I hadn't had enough (food) sometimes (in my other lives). In Paulinne's day people sometimes get weary with the struggle, don't they? People take their own lives, you get drug casualties and suicides. That is very rare these days, because there would be absolutely no reason for it. You wouldn't be in that dreadful place in your head …

Ye: Are any of the beings in your present life?

I consider my friends around the bed … yes. And you are

there, Ye, you're more interested in music than mosaics. We have theramin-type instruments and lasers to make sounds—all sorts of things. We were friends. Really good friends, but we pair bonded with other people. I've been on my own for a while since my partner died.

Because people had a lot more time together and did a lot more communal activities together, friendships went deeper. We were more evolved in a spiritual sense. We all loved one another and we were very much in harmony with one another—all the people in the community. Anyone who didn't fit in would have gone off to find another community where they did fit. The community was made up of people who had loved one another one way or another in other life times, which is why we were very harmonious.

Ye: How does that life relate to your present life?

As Paulinne I've got the seeds of things now—the inner work and artist/creative activities. I like making mosaics and putting things together, so it relates like that. I like music, I love the inner world and traveling, I like knowing what the news is—I'm always checking the BBC website for news late at night. And I've always been interested in the cosmic beings, the brothers and sisters on other worlds. I've found a pattern of contact and a prebirth contract to help humanity wake up to the fact that we are not alone.

Ye: go forward to after the evening meal.

There is a news broadcast about ETs. They measure our development. Like we measure a growing child's height, they've been measuring our collective consciousness and how it is upping its frequencies. We've passed some big marker.

There's a celebration! We shriek and whistle and clap and hug. Humanity's success is a natural completion of things for "soul me" because I've been engaged in this through many incarnations. It's like my soul can bow out and say my work here is done!

Then the music starts.

It's gorgeous and I can feel my body relaxing.

I go traveling … I meet some of my ET friends in my astral body state, and then I come back. I'm aware of being back in my body in the communal room but I can see angels and guides;

they've come like they said they would.

An angel takes hold of each hand and they lift me up out of my body … take me up above Earth, and I know that's the last time I will ever leave that body.

I'm going up into higher levels. I'm in a lot of light. I'm moving up through a lovely warm, living light. I'm going Home. Back to the Divine.

Ye says that's as far as I need to go.

It is time to consider if there is any healing to be done.

I have to make a real effort to pull myself back. It was a lovely life and a lovely end—and I'm so glad I saw the time line where I didn't drown. With Ye's help I release energy from my feet, chest, and throat from the running-for-my-life event, and I rebalance with a golden-white light. When we finish I visualize floating up my body, through my crown, back to the cave bed, back to Poseidon.

Poseidon is laughing. "One of my waves nearly got you!" he says. He said he held it back but he needed to give me a scare because I was getting too careless.

I thank him. That's when I notice Silver Brother is here.

I haven't seen Silver Brother in the inner world for a long time. He's a wolf I raised from a cub long ago, my friend and hunting companion from a lonely Native American past life. Love is a magnet that draws souls together through space and time, and Silver is saying he was one of the wolves who lived in the sculpture park. He was an animal friend of mine in Arwinn's life, too, and I'm giving him a hug. There's something very reassuring about hugging an animal's body, isn't there? They've got such good hearts. He's saying, "Right, Boss, it's time to go up the steps!" He just wanted to come and say hello because he wasn't at the bed scene, and I might not have remembered he had been in the life. We'd said goodbye over breakfast in the sculpture garden.

I do as he says and visualize climbing the steps.

Ye counts me up from zero to ten.

And I return to present time.

Ye asks me what year it is.

I want to say 2020, instead of 2019—maybe it's a good sign —if I can't wait to get there!

There is one more session to do.

* * *

Discussing the life over a cup of coffee afterward, Ye and I consider some ethical implications at odds with our viewpoint today. Forced evolution via brain stimulation had been seen as a good thing, and they had a very practical approach to dead bodies, valuing the protein. It was hard to get our heads around that.

This time line has been stable for twenty years to my certain knowledge.

Although it was only AD 2300+ (and by the time I died AD 2400+), we had already begun loosening our identification with, and connection to, the physical body. Separating ourselves out from it each evening, when we did the music-induced dream traveling, and on the occasions when we traveled in our astral bodies through the machines to visit other places. If you remember chapter 7, eventually we will evolve to the point where we do not need physical bodies at all, when we live like angels, but with free will, after Earth has been claimed by the expanded, dying sun.

* * *

Well, I don't know why I'd been so eager to get into 2020 at the end of this session — because although it brought me my longed-for second book, *Holy Ice*, it brought nothing but trouble. A pandemic swept across the globe. Shops were closed, travel was severely restricted, personal freedoms were eroded, and people around the world died because the virus attacked their lungs.

The authorities had clamped down hard to silence Extinction Rebellion's activities, and instead the news was filled with reports of the pandemic; COVID-19 was a virus that jumped species from bats, and mutated. The outbreak began in China at the end of 2019. The germ labs in Wuhan had been researching bat viruses, but it was Wuhan's food market that the authorities blamed.

As humankind suffered Earth began healing. The restrictions forced upon us to slow the spread of the virus benefited Earth. We were locked down at home and thus stepping lighter on the planet. Demand for oil plummeted, aeroplanes were grounded, and polluted air in the cities cleared.

Pegasus was trampling us hard.

Let's pick up the threads of the story and return to July 2019

- Chapter 13 -
Completion: Session 3, July 23, 2019

July 2019 brought the fiftieth anniversary celebrations of the Apollo 11 mission launch that put man on the moon. Tuesday night of the anniversary week was a full moon, a blood moon, and a partial lunar eclipse—it was Tuesday, July 16, and that Tuesday was a night to be noticed. I might have known something would happen.

At lunchtime that day Ye had returned home from walking Hadrian's Wall, the old Roman Wall that once protected the Roman province of Britannia from wild Scottish tribes of blue-tattooed Picts. We live near the Wall.

Although Ye had been away for a week, before he'd set out he'd done the session in the previous chapter, and now he was back we were planning the final regression for *Divine Fire*.

So Ye was back, and after a few days' rest we do the final session.

I find myself on the same beach.

Turquoise sea to my left, trees to my right, and lovely white sand.

There are pretty little shells in the sand this time and a blue sky arching overhead scattered with fluffy white clouds. It is midday. A gentle breeze stirs the fronds of the palm trees. It is very warm and relaxing, I seek the shade of the trees, and as I walk toward them I see small white flowers and pink hibiscus blooms.

I lie down, and absorb the beauty and energy of the lovely place.

Ye tells me to walk along the beach and contact my guardian angel.

She is in the trees. Helena appears big again today. She says she needs to be to keep me safe, and we walk together to find the cave. This time I see an inviting lake beside the cave. It attracts me and I decide I'm going to go down to the lake. The sun is sparkling on the water and the breeze is rippling its surface. I dip my toes in, it's lovely and warm and makes me feel very peaceful. Like I could just dissolve out into the water and become one with the universe … (The relaxation had been very deep when we first started. I was in deep.)

I glimpse mountains beyond. It's a bigger island than I thought. There's a smoking volcano … Helena is saying it's nothing to worry about but we might come back here another time.

Ye tells me to pause for a moment. Because before we go any further he needs to do the invocation: it's the point where we always ask God, our guides, and the Archangels for help and protection, that everything may be in accordance with the will of God. (I often don't mention this in the transcripts because I don't want to bore people with too many details of the process, but it is important. And for some reason I feel I have to mention it now.)

I walk into the welcoming waters of the lake.

Ye counts down from ten to zero.

And I walk down to the bottom of the lake with my angel. I see fish and weed. I'm standing on sand and there are some big rocks and boulders here. Helena says the volcano threw them out a long time ago, and that's how they got here.

Ye tells me to contact the spirit of the lake.

This time the guardian of the inner world is a mermaid, Poseidon's queen, Amphitrite. She is beautiful and wears a small golden crown, a diadem with shells on it. She opens the lake bed and she will guard it until I return.

Ye counts me down further, and I'm floating through the lake bed, down through my crown and down into my own body to find the main area linked to the experience I need to see. I scan through. It's my hands. The emotions connected to the experience are wonder, and a little bit of fear.

I sink into the feelings so a picture can come clear.

Ye tells me to look at my feet and to tell him what I see.

I see my own feet, bare feet, in bed.

Ye asks me how old I am at this point.

I'm seventy-one. This is me now. I'm wearing my new nightdress (one I bought while Ye was away on the Wall). This has to be a recent experience.

Ye: Are you alone?

No. You are there.

Ye: Is Ye asleep?

Yes.

Ye asks what the time is.

2:30 a.m.

Ye asks if I'm awake.

Well … I'm at that drifting-off-into-sleep point, when I'm half awake but I'm hardly awake.

Ye: Are you aware of something?

No …

But …

They are waiting for me to go to sleep.

Ye: Who?

Aliens, extraterrestrials … They can tell from my implants whether I'm awake or asleep; the implants give off a reading.

Ye: Do you know where your implants are?

They're in my head, feet, hands … some in my spine. They are not all physical. Most are in the subtle bodies. And they belong to different sets of ETs—all Galactic Federation ETs, so they know about one another. But if they were looking for me and needed to find me, they can only find me if I've got their particular implanted "tag." Most of the implants are locating devices, because they want to keep me safe—a lot of resources go into having their people here. They put a fair bit of effort into keeping their people/agents/resources—monitors—safe. They are for our benefit.

They're waiting for me to drop off to sleep.

I have. There are two of them in the room now.

Ye: Describe them.

They are very thin and gangly. They are humanoids, I'm not aware of having seen them before. They could be robotic, just sent to collect me.

Ye: How did they get into the room?

They came in on a beam. They are not terribly solid. They're what you call an "energy being." They are beings—it's the suit thing they are wearing that makes them look robotic. They have a protective outfit on.

Ye: Are they tall or small?

Bigger than me, about seven feet tall. Very gangly. Thin.

Ye: What are they doing?

Gathering me up … Hmmm … I'm asking myself if it's a physical or an astral contact this time. It's astral. They're just taking my astral body. They needed me to go to sleep, and then before my astral body can detach and go wandering in the astral realms, they've come to take me somewhere.

Ye: So your physical body will remain in bed?

Yes. If anyone were to look in the bedroom I would appear to be in bed, because my body is, but I've gone. My body mustn't be disturbed until I come back, so you've been put into a deep sleep … so has the cat. (Ye and Fizzy the cat are the only ones in our house tonight.) The cat has been given a very compelling and interesting dream, cycling through its happiest memories. ETs can see the emotional weighting on memory. They can use your memories to pacify you.

Ye: Are they still in the room?

Yes … they are lifting me out of my body. A beam comes in through the window … and we are just floating up the beam … out through the window, and I pass through the glass as if it were mist, over the garden, over the roofs of the houses outside … and up into the dark night sky … stars … it's a big moon.

Ye: Are there other people being gathered?

I can only see me but that doesn't mean anything, because I'm sort of asleep. I've got a very dulled awareness. I'm just aware of them really … I feel not exactly zombiefied but asleep (and my voice was strange on the tape, sleepy, slow, deep, throughout this entire experience).

We are arriving now at a craft. There's a threshold area, like a platform. I'm pulled onto that … and there's a very brightly lit open hatch, a doorway—an entrance area. I'm pulled into that and bathed in light, a light that will kill bacteria (I don't know what bacteria would be on my astral body)—but I'm cleansed at this point by a light bath in different color lights. Oh, it's for them as well, in case they picked up anything.

We are bathed in light here and then we go on.

A scanning device goes over us to check we are "clean."

Ye: Are they still carrying you? Or are you walking?

They are carrying me. I'm in a sleep pose. I'd turned over on my side in bed, and that's how I am now. They are carrying me along this corridor.

Ye: Are there any other beings in the corridor?

Yes. Lots of activity.

Though my eyes are shut I have awareness of the situation and I can sense the activity. Traveling is very smooth—they are standing on a "conveyor belt," but it's an energy stream. There are lots of different energy streams in the base part of this corridor, and lots of dimensional overlaps here. Beings hop on to the particular energy stream that is keyed to their vibration, and helper and enabler beings and the beings they are bringing in just whiz along. We are going at quite a speed. This must be a very big craft.

The energy streams terminate at a big gathering place.

… a circular place with lots of beings in it. Like a theater auditorium.

Ye: Lots of different beings?

Yes, I get a sense that is so. They are not particularly wanting me to know what's going on. There are animals here, too.

Ye: Do you know why they don't want you to know?

They got disturbed when there was too much bleed-through, when their activities were affecting the conscious level of our reality, back in the 1990s and around the turn of the century. They have had to backpedal on the bleed-through. It contravened some regulation about interference on other worlds. They'd overstepped the mark. That's why the alien thing has all sort of died a death, and we are not seeing images of aliens in ads on the TV like we did after the *X Files*. (And the *X Files* were popular because people hungered for knowledge. Though their contact experiences were buried in the subconscious, they could sense them.)

Ye: So this gathering, is that where you're being taken?

Yes. I'm wanted for this gathering. I'm being put in the equivalent of a seat, but it's a booth or pod with translation devices, perceptual screens, perceptual imaging, and hearing adjustment devices so I can understand what's going on.

They are waking me up. I'm thinking, "Flipping heck!" and "What's going on?!!!"

The perception filters are because they don't want to scare people. I'm perceiving it as being in a theater, as if there are tiers of seats and a central stage area because I'm familiar with that format.

Ye: So you're in the audience?

Yes, it's like I'm in a box in one of the balconies.

Ye: So you're going to witness something?

Yeah ... some sort of information briefing session.

Ye: Right.

Sometimes the experiences are more interactive when you are wide awake, or even physically present, but this is very subdued.

Ye: So you're going to be given some information?

I feel like I've been tranquilized. I couldn't move if I wanted to. But I am aware. I have been very deeply relaxed. You know when you're asleep you have a natural sleep paralysis because your body doesn't want to injure itself? It's like that. I can't really move, but I'm comfortable now I've been brought up to awareness, and these perception filters will help me understand what's going to happen and what I'm seeing or ... (hearing).

Ye: Are the two beings that brought you still with you?

Still with me. They tell me they will stay with me throughout the experience and then take me back. They tell me I am not abandoned.

Ye: Do they say what the experience is going to be?

They're saying watch and listen and you'll like it.

(I laugh.) It's a celebration.

Ye: Celebration?

Mmm … I don't know what they are celebrating. I'm here because I'm part of it, one of the workers … that's why they are wanting to share something.

Ye: Right.

I get the impression this is going to be repeated in many places around and above the Earth, and for many people. It's a bit of a thank-you, an assessment, like when you've had your essay marked at school.

There is a circular white central area where something is going to happen …

There's a beam come up now. You know in that future life there was a laser/hologram beam where people sat in a circle? Well, it's something like that. I expect that was ET technology … There is sound and light and pictures now. At the moment it's just showing patterns and I can't decode the patterns. They are saying that's because I've not got my perception filters adjusted.

Ye: How do you do that?

The booth I'm in has got a screen. I see through the screen to this laser display and they've got to calibrate the screen. It is an interdimensional thing; they need to adjust its frequency, because it's not just humans that go in these boxes—so they are adjusting it to human perception levels now.

That's getting better.

It was looking like interference and static before. It is showing pictures now.

Oh dear … Pictures of devastated rainforests in the Amazon where illegal loggers have been; pictures of dreadful plastic in the sea. Oh dear … melted glaciers; scorched areas of growing desert—*it's all our sins*—how we have failed in the stewardship of Earth. Hmmm … they say they are outlining the problem, the mountains of toxic rubbish we generate, toxins that are leaching out into the seas and the water, the air—what we did to the land with our modern farming techniques. They are outlining the scale

191

of the disaster. They say the scale isn't completely apparent from where we are, on Earth in 2019.

We are going to find out it is more widespread and more devastating than we imagine.

However—there is hope!

Also, I'm being told the Earth has been through some very terrible times in the past. Times which were nothing to do with us—asteroid strikes, even alien wars. You know some aliens have thrown wars on our planet?!!! Even before humans were there. They triggered some Ice Ages and have done all sorts. I knew vitrified sand had been found in deserts which looked like the result of a nuclear explosion, but really … The cheek of it![82]

But Earth survived.

The message is: Earth is very strong. But we have behaved despicably and we should have known better. And it is unbridled greed and the polluter not paying which really has to change. So a lot of souls have been drafted in to bring a turnaround, and that's the young people we have today, like the people leading and joining the Extinction Rebellion protests.

There have always been people who knew things were wrong, those who have supported Greenpeace and Friends of the Earth, … hippies, but they have been voices crying in the wilderness until now. Society hasn't taken anything on board until now. Now it's becoming much more mainstream because there are a lot more people involved in the prevention and turnaround programs that these ETs are stimulating.

They are trying to stimulate us to save ourselves.

They can't save us, it would break a lot of Federation treaties. They can't interfere beyond subliminally educating. Education is smiled on … and they have been doing that, for a long time. Lots of people have nighttime contact like I'm having now—have briefing sessions—and fragments of their experiences may bleed-through afterward into their dreams.

We had to be terrified by what we'd done.

All the nuclear angst in the 1950s and 1960s, we haven't half

---

82 For example, in Mongolia's Gobi Desert, in Israel and Iraq, in the western Arabian Desert, and there's also Libyan desert glass.

let a genie out of the bottle there. And many people's nightmares about nuclear destruction that were common back then were the result of bleed-through from the scenarios they had been forced to watch on the craft. But it's not just the nuclear stuff, it's all sorts. We have behaved badly—but I'm being told we are not the only ones who behaved badly. This has been a common pattern. There are many ruined worlds, and that's why the ETs are here. They are trying to help us draw back from the brink of extinction.

The message is: if we went extinct the Earth would still be here. The surface conditions would be different. We might have devastated soil and climate, even exploded so much nuclear stuff that we shredded the atmosphere, losing most of it—as happened on Mars. And a lot of our water may have been jettisoned out into space by the explosions, and gone wandering through the solar system—because we have benefited from other worlds' water, when similar things have happened elsewhere. Frozen lumps of water regularly come into Earth's upper atmosphere, as meteors, and percolate down. We have benefited from Mars and Maldek's water. It is one reason why we have such a beautiful planet. We have had more than our fair share of atmosphere and water.

Well, that's the bad stuff. The pictures are changing.

The ETs are very pleased with how our young people are reacting—embracing a massive vegan movement, while vegetarianism has never been so popular (because of the massive methane and carbon footprint of eating meat). It's a celebration because a lot of people are doing good work on the levels of change. A lot of the souls who have incarnated are remembering their missions and are being quite fearless.

The ETs have these assessment times on a regular basis, when they look at what's happening, and where the collective consciousness of humanity is registering. And we are lifting out of greed a little. You know, when you realize you can't eat money after you've poisoned the last fish? The Native Americans told us that a long time ago, but it is making sense to more and more people now.

Ye: are there any instructions specifically for you?

193

The instructions are: listen and record, that this is for the end for the book. I was instructed to write the book … throughout my life I've had help from inner guides, angels, and higher levels, and the culmination of all the help is my three books, *Spiritual Gold*, *Holy Ice*, and *Divine Fire*. They are time-tied. I always felt they should have happened sooner, but not so, I'm being given to understand now. If they'd happened earlier they would not have mentioned the Extinction Rebellion and that is important. They are meant for this time.

Anything else I achieve beyond this point is a bonus, and I'm to continue opening peoples' eyes to the fact that we are not alone. We have never been alone.

Ye: that's good—we've never been alone …

Because we are the result of a breeding experiment. ETs brought DNA to Earth, and the Earth forces (gravity, climate, the peculiar and unique systems of Earth and its maintenance entities) all put their stamp on the DNA, and on the forms that developed from it. But it was all gifted to Earth from the stars and so there is a wide spectrum of beings on the planet. There are beings on Earth we don't even know about because they are in higher dimensions and we can't see them.

We've never been alone—because we're an experiment that is being monitored. Well, we do that in laboratories, don't we? We start a culture in a petri dish and we monitor it, whether we're looking for new antibiotics or whatever. We start something off and see how it develops. Well, that's happened with Earth. The DNA that evolved into Earth's intelligent life forms then got tweaked further, and after a few extra DNA infusions, lo and behold you have us! And we're not the end of the process.

No, we've never been alone and we're not likely to be.

All those astronomers going, are we alone?!!! Every time they get a bigger telescope they say, "Oh, the universe is bigger than we thought …" It would be beyond a miracle if we were alone.

Ye: Is anything else happening with the presentation?

It has been showing us that things are very, very serious. But there are new shoots of hope growing with the young people. The young people seem to be picking up their missions, taking up the race to save humankind—so there are great signs of hope.

We have begun to see there could be a way out of the burning building that we have accidently set on fire. Let's hope we don't asphyxiate and burn to death before we get to the way out. But they are celebrating because there is a chance that we may. That we could pull back from the brink of disaster and things *could* lead to a Golden Age. There was the one in the last regression, but there are various alternative potential Golden Ages, not just that one. The beautiful possibilities of the future are ever changing, but we are grounding a wider variety of more positive outcomes than looked possible at one point. That is good news. We can't be complacent, we still have a lot of work to do—but, hey, the door to escape is open, we just need to see it and go through!

And there is so much that ordinary people can do in their everyday lives, when they stop supporting the fossil fuel industries and think about the choices they are making. We can start avoiding plastic, and we can start making wiser choices, and things will get better, and then we will find our way out. It's not that plastic is evil, but it is evil in the wrong place.

Plastic has many uses and should be recycled in a much better way than the pathetic attempts that have happened so far. It's actually a fabulous resource and there needs to be proper research into recycling it, and the amazing things it can make. I think there is a lot of science around the corner that we may be helped with (by the ETs) for that.

Some discoveries happen in dreams, like the inventor of the sewing machine who saw spears in a dream and they inspired the needles for the machines. Our great scientists have had a lot of insights in dreams—because that is one way we are easily influenced, in our dream state. Like in this experience I'm having now with the ETs, I'm only semiconscious. I'm conscious enough to log information I'm being given, but I won't have conscious memories of it when I wake up in the morning. But it will influence me from my subconscious.

Ye: Is there any more information for you?

The big thing is the message of hope.

We have turned a corner. The epidemic of suicides among young people is of great concern and was very worrying to the ETs, because a lot of those young people were key people in the mission to get us to open our eyes and wake up from sleep walking to disaster. But the stigma with mental health issues is coming away now, and being lifted, so that's a good thing and it will help troubled young people. It's been a very hard time to be young. They've got pressures that we never had—bullying and trolling on social media, and false images of beauty with photo-shopped pictures—dreadful rubbish that teaches you to hate yourself. We need to accept ourselves as we are, not berate ourselves for "flaws," which are our unique qualities. We need to celebrate ourselves. But social media is not all bad. On Facebook I came across this:

> "In a society that profits from your self doubt,
> liking yourself is a rebellious act."

(I laugh) and that is exactly what we need to do! Like ourselves! It is a rebellious act that can only bring good.

And that's part of the Extinction Rebellion, loving ourselves and laughing at things. Laughing at the status quo, laughing at the old values because they are so wrong. Big po-faced institutions do not like to be laughed at and poked fun at. And laughter is one of the most powerful weapons young people (and we) have. (And as I say this to Ye I have tingles running down my legs.) Laughter is the sunshine of the soul and the music of God. It's a really high-energy thing. You need intelligence to see the humor in things, and we need to use that God-given intelligence and we need to laugh, laugh at all the wrong stuff and let it shrivel up in shame and crawl away and die. (I have to laugh here because I've got so carried away.) And then there's room for something else: new businesses, new ways of doing things, new ways of seeing ourselves, new ways of fashion, new ways of eating, new ways of everything. And then we will have a future, and then we will have so much more happiness in the world. (And I still have tingles going up and down my legs at this point.)

So really that's it. It's a crisis party, but it is a party and we need to laugh! A really big laugh! No point in being all po-faced and miserable. It's a hoot! That is what we've come here for. Laughter is a fabulous healing thing. I have heard there's people healed themselves from cancer by watching funny films back to back and laughing—that's not what we're sold, is it?—to just laugh at things. And that's what we need to do. It's not all about working hard, doing endless worthy things, and going to bed exhausted, it's about seeing with new eyes and laughing! And that will energize us and shrivel the opposition.

Ye: Any other information you need to have?

Ask me why there are animals here.

Ye: What animals?

Horses, dogs, cats, birds. I'm not interacting with them because they are in their own booths … It's because all the life forms on the planet deserve to know what's happening, not just us. The ETs don't differentiate, to them the animals are as important as we are. We think we're top dog, don't we? But there's more of a collective consciousness with animals, and so they have some representatives of their species here, because the information will feed back into their group soul. They have their own perception filters, and they're getting their own information; the planetary energies are evolving and so all the beings on the planet are evolving too.

The message is: mankind is up on its hind legs thinking it's the only thing that matters but that's not true. We're a very big danger to the other species we're annihilating. We might think the Extinction Rebellion is about preventing us being extinct—but we're only one part of the jigsaw. Earth was quite happy before we evolved and Earth will be here after we've gone—well, that's if we get it wrong! (If we get it right we will still be here, and we will evolve to the pitch of angels, as it says in chapter 7.)

So—the situation is dire but there is hope.

Laughter is the weapon.

It doesn't half enrage people when you laugh at them. Only the bad people, because good people would simply join in with you and go, "You're right!" So it's a bit of a litmus paper test, really, laughter.

Ye: Is there anything else?

It is time to come out of the booth where I've been.

I'm being carried back to the "conveyor belt," which is now going the other way ... Beings are leaving the gathering space and I'm whizzing along to the light shower. I mustn't take anything back with me that I might have picked up here. Then it's back to that landing stage area ... Then ... Wheeeeeeeeeeeee ... floating down a beam ... Ssssshoooo passing through the atoms and molecules of the window ... and into the bedroom.

I am above my body and then gently eased into it.

The gangly energy beings make a ringing sound and that puts my astral body into my physical body and connects it.

They float off up the beam through the window, and they're gone.

And I know I wake up soon after, and visit our small ensuite bathroom to pass water. That's always a good way to make sure you are back in your body.

Ye: What day was it? You said the moon was big ...

It was last Tuesday, when you got back from the Wall.

We had our information, and there was no healing needed. I strengthened my aura with pink energy and then it was time to float up my body, through my crown, to the open lake bed and back to Poseidon's queen.

Amphitrite closes the lake bed.

She tells me it's the laughter of women that men are frightened of. We have been taught not to use that power, but now it is time. We don't have swords but we do have laughter, and it is a very powerful and a very positive weapon.

Nobody should be too big and too high and mighty to laugh at themselves—not queens or heads of banks or anything. I can imagine that the Dalai Lama could laugh at himself. It is a sign of a great soul and of great spiritual attainment to be able to laugh at yourself and not feel your ego shrivel.

I thank her.

Ye counts from zero to ten.

And I visualize myself walking up from the lake bed and come back into present time.

Ye checks what year I think it is.

2019, Tuesday, July 23rd.

Then I curl up under the blanket and he goes to make coffee. Bless him. I am a lucky woman. (For having such a lovely husband—not for having alien contact—that's exhausting and encourages my insomnia.)

- Chapter 14 -
Butterflies and Crystals!

We have stoked the fire and now we find ourselves inside the Creator's kiln, rough clay vessels that we are. We longed for the transformation only fire can bring. The world is heating up around us. Global warming and climate devastation is the test. Can we emerge from the divine fire of the kiln transformed, as beautiful as porcelain? Can we unite to save our world, or will we fall apart, just brittle shards to be tossed aside—another failed experiment from the Creator's kiln of life?

There is something we can do.

In fact, there is a lot we can do.

No one is too small to make a difference.

Years ago I read a science fiction story, where time travelers visiting the past accidentally step on a butterfly. Only a tiny creature, but that small action in time resulted in a big difference later. On their return home, they found their world changed. You are an important part of the web of life, and just like those time travelers what *you* do counts. If we all do what we know in our hearts to be right, we will make a tremendous difference to the future. Even little things, like signing petitions, might make all the difference.

And in addition to the crystal skulls already mentioned, there are mountains of planetary crystals available to us that can help bring the transformation we need. Crystals make up most of Earth's rocky crust. Crystals are stitched into the very fabric of our reality. Some are nearly as old as Earth herself. Earth's heart is a giant iron crystal.[83] We are surrounded by crystals! And they are even inside us, calcium crystals make up our bones and our bodily fluids readily crystallize out. We have a natural connection with crystal—and it is time now to activate the planetary crystals. To switch them on.

Let me explain.

Like the skulls, they are commanded by thought.

In our meditations and prayers we could activate and direct them to break up the old thought forms of fear, lack, poverty, disease, limitation, and greed that are crusted around the planet. We could replace old thought forms that are polluting Earth's aura with golden visions of the future. Don't underestimate thought. Toxic thoughts can corrode a human body and bring disease

---

83 Ronald Cohen and Lars Stixrude of the Carnegie Institute of Washington discovered it in 1995 with a sophisticated computer model of the Earth's inner core. The outer core of Earth, about two-thirds of the way to the center is molten iron, but deeper, at the inner core, the pressure is so great that iron solidifies, even though the temperature is believed to be hotter than the surface of the sun. The heat and pressure make ideal conditions for crystal growth, and a puzzling anomaly in the seismic data fits the research: properties of this crystal structure explain why sound waves travel faster when they are moving parallel with the Earth's North/South rotational axis. The work was published in *Science* magazine.

and ill-health, both mental and physical. In higher dimensions, thoughts actually manifest, and many ETs simply make what they need with thought. Thought always comes first before anything happens. We use only a small part of our mental powers in normal life, but when we are united in a common purpose the power of our thoughts and visualizations is exponentially amplified.

It was during a past life session the year that Princess Diana died that I first came across the idea about our planetary crystals. My client had gone back to the memories of a Stone Age life in England, where she was playing a key role at a summer solstice festival. The people were celebrating the event at a gathering in an ancient stone circle, and the stones were very important to them.

Her people studied the stars and she made star maps, which she traded at the big equinox and solstice festivals. The festivals were for trade as well as for religious fertility rites, they were popular social events and people traveled long distances to be there. There was plenty of feasting. But there was another factor drawing the tribes to the stones. At certain times at the festival a blue light would beam down from above, enveloping those within the stone circle. The light brought knowledge, gave them information, educated them and taught them things. Blue beings in a craft hovering above the circle were responsible, and they acted like teachers to these early people. The information was received telepathically, and this was another reason why people flocked to the festivals. Knowledge is power, it gives you an edge when it comes to survival.

In the altered state of consciousness that happens during a regression session, time can be fluid, as it is in dreams. An entire life can be compressed into a session, and sometimes the past can be interactive with the present—especially where ETs are involved in a contact experience.[84] It was as if the blue humanoid beings who had communicated with her then, so long ago, were aware of the work we were doing that day and they gave me a message through her—so I have to confess that it is not my idea to activate our planetary crystals to help us, it was an idea that

---

84 The blue men are still with us. See Ardy Sixkiller Clarke's *Space Age Indians: Their Encounters with the Blue Men, Reptilians, and Other Star People.*

came from the ETs.

Later I couldn't help but wonder if there was a connection between them and the ancient Hindu deities Krishna, Shiva, and Rama, who also had blue skin. Hinduism tells us that Krishna spent his life protecting humanity and destroying evil … To the ancient people who could see them telepathically the blue beings must have seemed like gods. Makes you think …

At the end of the book there's a visualization (or it can be more like a prayer) for world healing. It is simple and just needs a few quiet moments. It will benefit you and the planet, by increasing your harmony and uplifting your mood. Meditation and prayer always does this, it calms us down, puts us in touch with the peace of our higher levels. It enables our spirit to reach down to us and blow the breath of the Divine into our soul and into our life.

All you need is an intention to help.

In any form of healing, intention is the key. Intention calls forth help from the angels and focuses our will. We can create anything if we set our minds to it, but we rarely have that focus. Daily life keeps it scattered. Together we could achieve something tremendous! Even doing it once would be good. It will switch on a light bulb in higher dimensions!

In 1981 Fountain International started in Brighton, a seaside town in England. From small beginnings—the first meeting was attended by twenty local healers—it has become a worldwide community healing project based on the simple concept that communities, like people, suffer dis-ease, and may be healed. There have been measurable effects, the crime rate dropped in Brighton when it started. They say, "By tuning one's thoughts to an agreed point of focus in one's own community for just a few moments of each day, it is possible to radically improve the health of the community, and ultimately, we believe, the health of the world." In Brighton they chose a local fountain as the focal point. It is called Old Steine, because it marks the center of an old stone circle of that name, the ancient megaliths of which are in the base of the fountain. Being an ancient stone circle the fountain is, of course, positioned on ley lines.

Fountain International has an on-line magazine, so if you are interested it is easy to find out more. As they say, healing is applied unconditional love, and we can all help as part of this silent revolution. Certainly, the discoveries of post-Einstein physics, and both astrophysics and subatomic physics present us with evidence that our every thought influences the quantum field.

Oh, yes, our thoughts are powerful.

The year 2014 saw the first Crystal Skull World Day, when meditations for peace and harmony were synchronized across the globe. They have happened every year since. Uniting our minds like this may be more important than any physical reuniting of any particular thirteen skulls ... and perhaps it really is that simple. That remembering about them, and acting on that remembrance, is the key to accessing our deepest wisdom. Details of the annual World Days and other skull events can be found at www. crystalskulls.com.

Visiting the beautiful clear quartz crystal skull I know as Ra Nan Sa is always a pleasure, and I was given a message to share,

"I foresee a coming together of the races of Mankind, united in a single cause—to overthrow the yoke of tyranny wheresoever it oppresses the human spirit. My children are awakening from the slumber of the ages where they lay lost in the dreams of matter, imagining themselves no more than part of the material world, deeming too precious the illusions of matter, and blind to their own spiritual heritage—their birthright of spirit with eternity as their playground.

"But now is the start of the awakening into joy. For now is the time come to begin again that which was started long ago. The cycles return and urge you to transcendence. Uplift your minds to joyful pursuits and kind and loving thoughts. Create your ideal future with your own minds, when they are firmly focused on that which is truly important—life, love, and joy—for gloomy thoughts will not save Mankind, but joy and loving brotherhood will. Let the sisters of the world take their place in the positions of power, and let the new energies streaming to your planet from the cosmos lift you all into the next way of being—being in the world, but not being consumed by it, nor consuming it in the endless search for meaning through consumption. There is no meaning in consumption, and unchallenged it has the capacity to consume your very soul, dissolving away your spiritual strengths and previous achievements, leaving the soul diminished.

"Know you are not your bodies, but that you are so much more—shining spirit, divine gold, born from the mind of God, the Great Creator of the heavens and all that is. Be at peace. Enjoy your birthright as shining, golden, spirit beings of love and bliss. The rest is shadows of misery, and illusions that can trick the unwary into blindness of their true nature. Let no one take your birthright from you."

The last word belongs to the Mitchell-Hedges crystal skull. This is the most famous of them all. It resides in America with its current guardian, Bill Homan. This crystal treasure has served humanity for so long and has had many names over the millennia. I knew it as Bah Ha Redo, and like the skull Ra Nan Sa, it feels like an old friend to me because I have had many dealings with it in past lives. I was lucky enough to have an hour to meditate with Bah when it was brought to Edinburgh, Scotland, and I asked it about our future. I was told that we are on the threshold of "The time the nations have waited for." That soon,

"The time arrives that the stars shine bright in the heavens and peace is come upon the nations. Be joyful and of good cheer. Join your energy to the joy that is to engulf humanity. Laugh, for joy is come into the world and into the lives of my beloved children. Let the sun shine into your world, and lighten it with a smile. For my children awake from the sleep of ages. Let it be a birthday party for humankind to come of age to join your cosmic brothers and sisters and take your place at the cosmic table to banquet. Joy and love will save the world."

Remember, we came here to be together at this incredible time on Earth. Through the infinite depths of love in our hearts we answered the call when it came. "Volunteers wanted for the crisis party on Earth," rang out and we said, "Put us down for that! You can count on us! Wouldn't miss this for worlds!" And so we came, and we've found the crisis all right, but we need to remember the party! It's our joy and laughter that will build the strongest immune system and the strongest bridge to enter a Golden Age.

And we can
We can make heaven on Earth.
If we choose.

Let this be a time traveler's butterfly of a book.
You and I are not too small to make a difference.
We came to make that difference.
This is our purpose.
Our soul's sacred mission.
Can you feel it?

It's time to stretch our wings!

Acknowledgments

To all the beings who have helped this book happen, especially:

Ye Min and Veronica Fyland, who regressed me and gave me words of wisdom along the way, and in Ye's case, photographs. Isabelle Crummie and Guy Needler, whose advice has always worked magic; Hana Kanoo and Julie Lomas, without you I would not have known about the ancient Bahraini temples and so much else; Michele Nocerino for the photograph of Sha Na Ra; and Bill Homann for photographs of the Mitchell-Hedges crystal skull; my wonderful editor, Debbie Upton; Dolores Cannon, who has been a guiding star for me over the years and without whom there would be no Ozark Mountain Publishing; Nancy Vernon and Brandy McDonald and all at OMP; and last but not least my magnificent butterfly power animal whose gift is to see the beauty and fragility of life,

Many, many blessings to you all and a very big thank you!

We did it!

Nourishing Your Future

Laugh! Pure sunshine for your soul.

Let the day flow through you—take things lightly.

Choose to feel joy—enjoy the oxygen in your lungs, the people in your life, and every mouthful of food.

Positive affirmations really help. "I am a lucky woman" works for me. I either laugh at the absurdity of it, or feel blessed—depending on what is happening, but either way I win. And I am creating more luck!

Create "home as sanctuary" to nourish *you*.

Enjoy the luxury of time to yourself—even ten minutes is enough to feed your soul with a little beauty. Perhaps through music that lifts your mood and inspires you: the music of your youth keeps you young, Gregorian chant clears your aura, harp vibrations harmonize your cells. Pop on a CD. Dance, sing (banish judgmental thoughts! This is only for you—all that matters is: does it feel good to you?)

Let the perfection of living flowers lift and harmonize you—have them around you, and use flower remedies (like the Dr. Bach flower remedies) to bring harmony to your thoughts and emotions. Feel peace and send thoughts of love and healing out into the world and to our future.

Counting your blessings brings contentment—and more blessings …

Go "green" when you can—when shopping, and while investing your money … Consider the ethics of your bank, because switching is easy.

Contribute to disaster funds (every little bit helps)—make

209

your love a visible and potent force in the world.

Days of joy—any excuse will do, celebrate being alive!

(And why not visit an ancient sacred site? Every country has them.)

Time and the Pattern of Our Incarnations

We have many lives. My books do not hold the complete pattern of my incarnations, just the tiny part relevant to *Spiritual Gold, Holy Ice, Divine Fire*.

Lives on other worlds are tricky to slot into the framework of Earth time because they may be conducted in other time tracks. Some time tracks have the ability to intersect with ours, while others run parallel, but at different speeds. Einstein pointed out that time is related to gravity, and as gravity varies enormously throughout the universe, so does time.

Time also varies according to the dimensions you are in.

Our divine self, our causal body, holds so much power that it may ray down into more than one body at a time: it is said we can have up to a dozen parallel lives[85] going on at any one moment, where all the life experiences flow back to enrich our soul. This has gone on throughout history and because of it we can have incarnations that seem to overlap. Time is no simple linear flow, though it carries us through our days.

The gap between incarnations is not fixed. We may enjoy a rest of a thousand years in the heavenly realms, but there are no rules, because it depends on the needs of the soul. A soul burning to reincarnate, or wanting to complete an interrupted incarnational mission, can return very quickly; suicides, accidental deaths, babies, and children may fall into this category. For example, a child knocked over by a car while playing in the street returned

---

85 This figure is in Guy Needler's *The Anne Dialogues*, and I've come across a similar figure in Ruth White's Seth books; Dick Sutphen, a leading American regressionist with whom I have studied, has researched parallels extensively and found them to be ubiquitous, and by no means a rare occurrence.

to the same parents the next time the mother conceived. Those not fussy about the location or choice of parents, but just needing to be here to do something, may go, "Oh, yes, he owes me a body because he killed me in a battle, so I'll have him as Dad!" This can speed things up, but such hastiness is often rued later, especially in the teenage years, when karma tends to resurface. Remember that even though you've forgotten it, there's always a good reason for a difficult relationship.

There are more people on the Earth right now than there's ever been before—and this is an argument often put forward to disprove reincarnation—as in *where have all the extra souls come from?* But it is because this is such a special time that we all wanted to be a part of it; and it has come about because:

Many of us have opted for a very short stay in the spiritual realms in order to be here.

Citizens of the galaxy have come here from other worlds, willing to undergo an Earth incarnation to help us with the task of shifting our time line into a more positive outcome.

We may have parallel lives going on of which we are not aware, and the parallels may be on the planet with us now.

And as you can see from the lives on the time line, we switch between incarnating as a man and as a woman depending on what we are seeking to learn. So no prizes for guessing what a sexist man incarnates as next—and you can imagine what's awaiting a racist, a bigot, or a greedy banker.

Time Line of the Lives in:
Spiritual Gold, Holy Ice, and Divine Fire

THE PAST

The lands of Mu and Lemuria sank beneath the Pacific Ocean in a cataclysm of fire. In the South Atlantic, lands perished, too, ending the first civilization of Atlantis. The crystal skulls had been taken north for safekeeping.

The last Ice Age ended and (North Atlantic) Atlantis repopulated after 10,000 BC.

AN-HARA, Bahrain
AHMET, Egypt
NONI / WAMA-MARMA, Atlantis
SAHAARA, Atlantis
ARLO / ARLOS, Atlantis
AYESHA, Atlantis
THE PLEIADIAN, Atlantis
ARMALCO, Atlantis

Destruction of the second Atlantean civilization by water in 3114 BC.

Remnants of the continent of Atlantis lingered on near Central America. This was the Archipelago Stage. The explosion of Thera (the Greek island of Santorini) wiped out the pre-classical world and the Minoan civilization on Crete in the middle of the 2nd millennium BC.

2nd millennium BC: AKBAR, Bahrain
Mid 1st century BC: JEREMIAH
Jesus is born in the Holy Land (BC changes to AD)
1st century: NADIA, the Holy Land
1st century: MARY, the Holy Land
2nd century: 330:29, Venus
5th century: MOVES LIKE THE CLOUDS, North America
5th/6th century: JOHANNES, Britain
7th century: AKBAR, North Africa
18th century: AGATHA, Montpellier, France
???: RONWEG, and various lives on other worlds
20th century: PAULINNE, England
2012 Winter Solstice: The Pegasus influence begins
2048 Winter Solstice: The Pegasus influence ends
AD 2098: MANANNAN, South America
AD 2300+: ARWINN, Scotland

THE FUTURE

Visualization and Prayer to Help Heal Our World

I use the terms "Creator," "God," and "Source" to mean the same divine being.

Please read a step then close your eyes and visualize the action happening. Then read the next step and close your eyes and visualize the next action taking place, and so on.

Phone off, get comfortable, close your eyes, and settle down into your prayer mode.

Picture God's light flowing down from the heavenly realms and surrounding you, keeping you safe.

Ask the Archangels Michael, Uriel, Gabriel, and Raphael and their legions of angels to help you with this healing.

Visualize yourself huge and the world small. See yourself pulling out old black energy from our cities and sacred sites and our lands as if it were no more than black ribbons. Heap these in the waiting arms of legions of angels, who are returning it all to Source to be transmuted back into pure divine energy.

Visualize the angels taking the "ribbons" away, just see them go.

Picture God's light beaming down and flowing around the world, healing and harmonizing everywhere it touches. See the light flowing into the energy grids and veins of the world, rebalancing and healing them and our sacred sites and our cities.

Now picture the light flowing down into Earth's rocky crust on which we live. And then light flowing into all the crystals of the rocky crust, from the tiniest grains of sand to the deep, deep crystals in crystal caves. Flowing down and down and flowing into Earth's great crystal heart.

Picture all Earth's crystals waking up.

Give them their purpose. Say: I will and command that all you planetary crystals be dedicated to the highest, to God our Creator. I will and command all of you to be self-cleansing, and to only respond to those of us who work for Light. I will and command all of you to lift the vibrations of the world and bring an increase in harmony.

Breathe in deep.

Breathe out and hold a note: oooooooooooooooh …

Picture the harmony of your pure note shattering crusted thought forms of greed and fear in Earth's aura, so the angels sweep it away, returning it to Source.

Then ask God to:

Deliver us now from the sins of the past and the wounds of the world. Cleanse our spirits and our souls and our lands.

Renew us. Renew us with the Creator's light, and may we be blessed, and may this land be blessed.

May the Eye of Heaven be open once more—and may God's light flow down into the world through it. May Divine Grace pour forth, bringing peace and harmony and healing, so that humanity may enter a Golden Age, a time when we live in harmony with the Earth and all its creatures. I accept that it is done.

I thank the angels. Amen. (So be it.)

Prayer is powerful. We matter. We influence matter. We can really make a difference.

Bibliography

Bishop, Karen. *The Ascension Primer*. USA: Booklocker. com, 2006.

Calleman, Carl John. *The Mayan Calendar and the Transformation of Consciousness*. Rochester, Vermont: Bear & Company, 2004.

Cannon, Dolores. *Keepers of the Garden*. Huntsville, AR: Ozark Mountain Publishing, 1993.

Cannon, Dolores. *The Convoluted Universe*. Huntsville, AR: Ozark Mountain Publishing, 2001.

Cannon, Dolores. *The Three Waves of Volunteers and the New Earth*. Huntsville, AR: Ozark Mountain Publishing, 2011.

Clarke, Ardy Sixkiller. *Space Age Indians: Their Encounters with the Blue Men, Reptilians, and Other Star People*. San Antonio, TX: Anomalist Books, 2019.

Cope, Julian. *The Modern Antiquarian*. London: Thorsons, an imprint of HarperCollins, 1998.

Extinction Rebellion. *This Is Not a Drill*. UK: Penguin, Random House, 2019.

The Holy Bible, rev. ed. Cambridge: Cambridge University Press, 1924.

Hopkins, Budd. *Missing Time*. USA: Balantine Books, 1990.

Icke, David. *Human Race, Get Off Your Knees*. UK: David Icke Books, 2010.

Lomas, Julie. *Comfy Slippers and a Cup of Tea*. UK: Light Tree Books, an imprint of The Light Network, 2013.

Mack, John E., MD. *Abduction: Human Encounters with Aliens*. Great Britain: Simon & Schuster, 1994.

Morton, Chris, and Ceri Louise Thomas. *The Mystery of the Crystal Skulls: Unlocking the Secrets of the Past, Present, and Future*. London: Thorsons, an imprint of HarperCollins, 1997.

Needler, Guy. *The Anne Dialogues*. Huntsville, AR: Ozark Mountain Publishing, 2016.

O'Leary, Brian. *Miracle in the Void*. Hawaii: Kamapua'a Press, 1996.

Rossetti, Francesca. *Psycho-Regression: A New System for Healing and Personal Growth*. London: Judy Piatkus, 1992.

Science. Journal.

Stray, Geoff. *Beyond 2012 Catastrophe or Ecstasy*. UK: Vital Signs Publishing, 2005.

Strieber, Whitley. *Communion*. London: Arrow Books, an imprint of Century Hutchinson, 1988.

Thomas, Andy. *The Truth Agenda*. UK: Vital Signs Publishing, 2009.

Thunberg, Greta. *No One Is Too Small to Make a Difference*. UK: Penguin, Random House, 2019.

Watkins, Alfred. *The Old Straight Track*. London: Abacus by Sphere Books, 1974.

About the Author

Paulinne Delcour-Min BA Hons, PGCE was born in Chester, England. She trained as an artist, ceramicist and art teacher before becoming interested in healing, which led her to study regression therapy. After raising her family she now lives by the sea in the North East of England with her husband, who is also a writer and therapist.

Paulinne has been a past life and soul therapist for over thirty years. During this time she has helped many people review and learn from their past lives in order to benefit their present one. Her passion for understanding her own previous lifetimes has led to an extraordinary journey which she shares with us through her books. Her regression work is influenced by shamanic traditions, and with the help of angels and inner guides her work encompasses a wide range of healing techniques.

Her years of experience have taught her that we all have inner treasures and that there is no need to fear death! Our souls are on a glorious journey through the dimensions of the universe, and we always come to planet Earth with a mission. For many of us who answered the call to be here right now, that mission is to help the future….

Paulinne can be contacted through her website:
www.paulinnedelcour-min.com